T0334579

Cambridge Elements ≡

Elements in Feminism and Contemporary Critical Theory
edited by
Jennifer Cooke
Loughborough University
Amber Jamilla Musser
CUNY Graduate Center
Juno Jill Richards
Yale University

NONBINARY

A Feminist Autotheory

Stephanie D. Clare
University of Washington

CAMBRIDGE
UNIVERSITY PRESS

CAMBRIDGE
UNIVERSITY PRESS

Shaftesbury Road, Cambridge CB2 8EA, United Kingdom

One Liberty Plaza, 20th Floor, New York, NY 10006, USA

477 Williamstown Road, Port Melbourne, VIC 3207, Australia

314–321, 3rd Floor, Plot 3, Splendor Forum, Jasola District Centre, New Delhi – 110025, India

103 Penang Road, #05–06/07, Visioncrest Commercial, Singapore 238467

Cambridge University Press is part of Cambridge University Press & Assessment, a department of the University of Cambridge.

We share the University's mission to contribute to society through the pursuit of education, learning and research at the highest international levels of excellence.

www.cambridge.org
Information on this title: www.cambridge.org/9781009278676

DOI: 10.1017/9781009278645

First published 2023

A catalogue record for this publication is available from the British Library.

ISBN 978-1-009-27867-6 Paperback
ISSN 2754-303X (online)
ISSN 2754-3021 (print)

Nonbinary

A Feminist Autotheory

Elements in Feminism and Contemporary Critical Theory

DOI: 10.1017/9781009278645
First published online: May 2023

Stephanie D. Clare
University of Washington
Author for correspondence: Stephanie D. Clare, sclare@uw.edu

Abstract: This autotheoretical Element, written in the tense space between feminist and trans theory, argues that movement between "woman" and "nonbinary" is possible, affectively and politically. In fact, a nonbinary structure of feeling has been central in the history of feminist thought, such as in Simone de Beauvoir's *The Second Sex* (1949). This structure of feeling is not antifeminist but indexical of a desire for a form of embodiment and relationality beyond binary sex and gender. Finally, the text provides a partial defense of nonbinary gender identity by tracing the development of the term in online spaces of the early 2000s. While it might be tempting to read its development as symptomatic of the forms of selfhood reproduced in (neo)liberal, racialized platform capitalism, this reading is too simplistic because it misses how the term emerged within communities of care.

Keywords: nonbinary gender, gender-critical feminism, transgender, trans social media, Simone de Beauvoir

ISBNs: 9781009278676 (PB), 9781009278645 (OC)
ISSNs: 2754-303X (online), 2754-3021 (print)

Contents

1 Trans Desire's Retroactive Birth

It is 1993, or thereabouts. I'm at the municipal pool of Westmount, arguably one of the most conservative neighborhoods on the island of Montréal, and I see them: an apparently white, flat-chested person, wearing an athletic bathing suit marketed to women, a bathing suit that covers their chest. They have long hair pulled back into a ponytail and narrow hips. "I think we are alike," sings the character who plays the young Alison Bechdel in the musical remaking of Bechdel's graphic memoir, *Fun Home* (2006). Bechdel recounts the moment when she first sees a person who, she claims, is unlike anyone she's ever seen before, someone with short hair, dungarees, and lace-up boots, someone who is strong, and, ultimately, the young Alison sings, handsome. The song is about growing up in a world where children are not granted images or narratives about gender-nonconforming people. As a result, Alison is perplexed. "I feel … I feel …," she sings, naming no clear feeling. These unfinished sentences lead to the next lines, which also highlight the character's lack of knowledge: "I don't know where you came from / I wish I did / I feel so dumb. / I feel …." Notwithstanding this confusion, the song ends in some apparent clarity and knowledge, "I know you. I know you. I know you."

In this narrative, contracted and confused affect becomes reframed as self-recognition, which is a misrecognition too. Alison does not know the person, even if she says she does. She is projecting herself onto them. But the song, crucially, is not only about identity and identification. It is also about a feeling that blurs identification and desire, and a feeling that José Esteban Muñoz can help us to understand as a utopian "insistence on potentiality or concrete possibility for another world" (2009, 1). Alison sings in amazement about the person's ring of keys, made extraordinary in Alison's vision. The song expresses astonishment in the person and their keys, a form of astonishment that helps Alison to "surpass the limitations of an alienating presentness" and that allows her to imagine "a different time and place," which is why she wonders where the person comes from (Muñoz, 2009, 5). In the song, the ring of keys comes to signify, much as Muñoz writes of a Coke bottle in a Frank O'Hara poem, "a vast lifeworld of queer relationality, an encrypted sociality, and a utopian potentiality" (6). The ring of keys is utopian. It promises "a futurity, something that is not quite here" (7).

When I saw them at the pool, I felt relief – even joy, possibility. I could become them. *Please, let me become them.* I want to watch them as they swiftly move through the water, completing lap after lap. I do not know them, but onto them I project a possible future and different forms of relationality. Misrecognition entangled with desire, a confused and contracted affect experienced in the form of intensity. I see their beauty. Their valor. They are a sight to behold – not in the characteristic distancing and objectifying of scopophilia, but in the wonder of connection. Euphoria, not only dysphoria.[1] Another social world is possible.

Sometime around the age of fourteen, I began binding my breasts. At the time, I didn't have the language of binding, and I developed the practice on my own. I liked to use masking tape. Standing in the family bathroom, in front of the large, wall-to-wall mirror, I'd wrap the tape around my chest, directly on my skin, over and again, each morning. The work felt like a ritual of self-assertion, neither self-hatred nor exactly self-care. I was making of myself as I wanted to be. I trained myself into a signature posture, as well: chest concave, rounded shoulders, head forward. I always wore sweaters.

Had anyone asked why I worked to hide my breasts (and no one did), I probably would have yelled at them to leave me alone (and this might explain why no one asked). My breasts were not something I was capable of talking about. I could think about them, though, lying awake in bed, at night. And it was simple: I did not want my breasts to be seen. But it was also more complicated: I did not want to be seen wearing a bra, especially by my parents, because it would give them the satisfaction that I had accepted my fate. Yet at the same time, I did not want to be seen not wearing a bra, either, because then, too, I would feel exposed. I did not want anyone to think that I was "blossoming," whatever that meant, into a "young lady." I was not a flower. I was not something to be looked at. I was not a vehicle for reproduction or for someone else's pleasure. I did not want to become a "woman." And finally, here it is: I did not want my breasts to be there. When I'd take the tape off every night, it would hurt a little, especially around the nipples, and that seemed right. My body, in developing breasts, had betrayed me. The pain was part of its punishment. When I was in my twenties, after suffering upper back pain and neck immobility from my poor posture, a physiotherapist diagnosed me with kyphosis, an excessively rounded thoracic curve most common among elderly adults. It still hurts, right now.

Throughout these years, the unspoken assumption, treated as reality itself, was that nothing could be done for me as I slowly shrunk into myself. It is cisnormativity that made it such that I thought that my body had to take on a certain form, that I had no choice but to accommodate that body and to tolerate it. It is the limited "transsexual" narrative that gave me no language to articulate myself either: I did not identify with "the opposite sex," so I thought I couldn't

---

[1] As Beischel et al. (2021, 3) explain, "gender euphoria" has received little attention in academic literature, but it has been a term prominent in trans and nonbinary communities, especially online, since at least 2001.

be trans, but I did not see myself in this "female sex" either. Other people's refusal to recognize my feelings and the challenge I had in finding a public language that could help me to articulate myself and find a social place was the result of hetero and cisnormativity, patriarchy, abandonment, and disregard.

All of this sounds like a story (my story) of a trans or nonbinary child, of a child living in a world they wish were different but that they can't quite describe. But here's the thing: that child as trans or nonbinary has only appeared recently, retroactively, in my encounter with trans and nonbinary people, publics, literature, and theory.[2] Previously, this (somewhat) same child was a proto-lesbian feminist, born through my reading, during my late teens, of Adrienne Rich (1994) and the subsequent reorganization of my life, future, and communities. These two narratives, these two children, build two different subject positions and, with it, two different political visions: on the one hand, a woman, on the other, a nonbinary position; on the one hand, the project of resignifying "woman," and on the other, the refusal of compulsory "womanhood." *So which one is Stephanie?*

But do I have to choose? Can we not do both, together?

2 Care on the Borderland between Feminist and Trans Thought

I write in and about the tense space between feminist and trans thought. I am not, however, interested in the question of whether trans women ought to have access to women's spaces or to services for women – the answer seems clear: yes. Unless we want to ground the category "woman" in an embodied essence (for instance the possession of XX chromosomes or of a vagina) – and we don't – it is only in displacing differences between women that trans women's presence appears as a threat. In fact, the exclusion of trans women produces phantasmatic sameness, including a perceived sameness of embodied form, which has never been a promising basis for the category "woman" in the first place.[3] Existence precedes essence, and "one is not born, but rather becomes, woman" (Beauvoir, 2011, 283).

Equally, I am not interested in developing a trans feminism, which is to say a feminism that serves all women, and especially trans women. This is not because I am against this project but rather because there already exist important versions of such praxis, including Emi Koyama's "The Transfeminist Manifesto" (2003) and Julia Serano's *Whipping Girl: A Transsexual Woman on Sexism and the Scapegoating of Femininity* (2007). Emma Heaney (2017)

---

[2] I am borrowing the framework of "retroactive birth" from Kathryn Bond Stockton (2009).
[3] For an elaboration of this argument, one that places anti-transgender feminism within the context of the investment in purity amongst first-wave white, middle-class feminists, see Hines (2019).

reads the work of Sylvia Rivera and Marsha P. Johnson in this vein, too, and to Heaney's detailed tracing of trans feminist thought (253–97), I would add Viviane Namaste's and Mirha-Soleil Ross's work, especially their focus on sex workers' rights (Namaste, 2009, 16–18).

Instead of these points of encounter, I want to address a different meeting of feminist and trans thought, a meeting similar to what in the 1990s was referred to as the Butch/FTM Border wars, or, framed less antagonistically, as the borderland between butch and trans masculine identification (Halberstam, 1998; Hale, 1998). This 1990s borderland has not disappeared, but to it, today, we might add another layer, which is the focus of this text: a feminist inhabitation of the category woman, on the one hand, and a nonbinary position on the other. This borderland, on which I currently live, is not new, though its prominence and visibility, as evidenced in the growing use and acceptance of they/them pronouns, is.[4] And from this borderland, here is what I want to argue: movement between "woman" and "nonbinary" is possible, not just strategically but also emotionally or affectively.

In making this argument, I suggest that we understand nonbinary both as an identity, which is to say a recognized, social position (or set of social positions) in the world with which one identifies, and as a structure of feeling, which is to say a set of repeated patterns of emotion that emerge in response to the social world. In fact, all genders might be understood as both identities and structures of feeling. While both "identity" and "structure of feeling" reference something that the history of Western thought might characterize as internality or selfhood, a structure of feeling, unlike an identity, need not be explicitly recognized (by the self or others) in order to exist. That is to say, a structure of feeling might be present when a corresponding identity is not. Insisting on the difference between a structure of feeling and an identity helps to navigate the borderland between "woman" and "nonbinary": the distinction clarifies how, for those assigned female at birth, the assertion of a nonbinary identity is certainly not or not only a political evacuation of the category "woman" but also the recognition of a mode of feeling, belonging, and pleasure, to use Cameron Awkward-Rich's framework (2017). Likewise, insisting on the distinction between structures of feeling and identity clarifies how a feminist inhabitation of "woman" is not simply political but also, potentially, the assertion of a feeling, a sense of belonging, or a mode of finding pleasure. In other words,

---

[4] For instance, to give two high-profile examples, in 2017, *The Associated Press Stylebook* was revised to allow for the use of the singular "they," including to reference people who identify as neither male nor female. That same year, *The Chicago Manual of Style* followed suit, adopting the singular "they" both as a substitute to the generic "he" and to refer to a person who does not identify with gender-specific pronouns.

the existence of a nonbinary structure of feeling for those assigned female at birth is not a refusal of the social position of woman because feelings in themselves are not forms of refusal. But feelings might lead to refusal: the assertion of a nonbinary identity for those assigned female at birth is both a refusal of the social position of woman and the recognition of a structure of feeling.

I owe the phrase "structure of feeling" to Raymond Williams's 1977 *Marxism and Literature*. Williams argues that too often the social is understood in the past tense: the social is that which is always already formed. To this approach to the social, Williams seeks to add a dimension of experience that remains social but is lived in the present tense. Such present-tense consciousness, "what is actually being lived, and not only what is thought is being lived," is not "fully articulate" and yet exerts "palpable pressures and set[s] effective limits on experience and action" (132). "Structures of feeling" are complex and can be contradictory. They are expressed in the "affective text of consciousness and relationships: not feeling against thought, but thought as felt and feeling as thought" (132). We find structures of feeling in patterns of "impulse, restraint, and tone" (132). They have the property of the emergent and embryotic: that which is present and exerts force, but that which is not completely articulated and not quite taking the form of something fixed and fully present. The feelings are "structures" in that they often emerge "as a set, with specific internal relations" (132). Though structures of feeling are often "taken to be private, idiosyncratic, and even isolating," Williams argues that they are in fact shared ways of feeling in a particular historical moment, ways of feeling that emerge in relation to that historical moment, as a response to that moment, and also as part of that moment, as well (132).

I enter the borderland between woman and nonbinary as someone steeped in feminist and queer thinking, structures of feeling and points of identification, but also as someone invested in the project of trans liberation, who has only more recently spent time with trans thought. This is a dangerous place to be writing for at least three central reasons. First, there is a long history of feminist and queer scholarship turning to trans topics to extract theories of gender and sexuality that do not serve trans people. This scholarship often figures trans people as dupes to medicine or to gender itself (unlike the supposedly enlightened feminist/queer scholar), and the scholarship does not center trans people, trans thought, and trans cultural production.[5]

---

[5] For important examples of this critique of feminist and queer (and feminist queer) thought, see Prosser (1998, 21–60), Rubin (1998), Namaste (2000), Stryker (2004, 212–215), Namaste (2009), Heaney (2017), Benavente and Gill-Peterson (2019, 111); Chu and Drager (2019, 103–116); Chen (2019, 34–38).

Second and relatedly, in acknowledging that I have only more recently turned to trans studies, I am framing transness as new or recently "discovered." Such framing has the twin dangers of, on the one hand, treating trans people as exotic others to be gazed at and scrutinized (often with the goal of extracting "knowledge" about gender) and, on the other hand, placing a question mark over trans existence itself.[6] As Jules Gill-Peterson argues, when transness is presented as new and therefore without the ontological weight of history, it becomes, at worst, a possible and passible fad and at best, a figure of futurity with no being in the present (2018a, 2).

The final reason why the position from which I write is thorny is that I think it is fair to say that I am writing as someone who has experienced and still experiences gender dysphoria but, also, as someone who has found some level of resolution to this experience through feminism, especially lesbian and queer feminism.[7] I just framed my experience in the psycho-biomedical language of gender dysphoria in an honest attempt at describing it. But turning to this language is also symptomatic of the continued ways in which authenticity and realness have been called upon to limit and control transness. On the one hand, I seek authenticity by turning to this discourse to provide an authoritative term that describes my experience and that places me in a "true" relationship to transness. And yet, this psychological, biomedical discourse, as well as the requirement to "prove" "realness," needs to be called into question for both have been used to regulate transness (i.e., see Spade, 2006). In any case, to say that I have found some resolution to gender dysphoria in feminism can easily be misconstrued as an argument against transition. One central refrain of "gender-critical feminism" (also known as "trans-exclusionary feminism") is the argument that what trans people need is, simply, a good dose of feminism.[8] In this view, trans medicine and identity accommodate rather than challenge gender norms. Instead of resignifying the meaning of a female body and therefore transforming how the category "woman" is understood (as has been a key feminist project), trans people and politics reassert the importance of gender, "mutilating" bodies to fit and reproduce, as best as possible, patriarchal norms. To insist then that I have found some resolution to gender dysphoria in feminism appears to be promoting this logic even if this is not my intention.

While I acknowledge the dangers of writing from my position, there is something worthwhile in writing from this vantage point, something that

---

[6] For a foundational argument about such exoticism, see Stone (1992, 163).

[7] As Patrick Califia put it in 1997, "There are many levels of gender dysphoria, many aberrant accommodations other than a sex change. Feminism, for example" (6).

[8] For examples of this argument, see Jeffreys (2014) and Shrier (2020). For an overview to gender critical feminism, see Hines (2019).

would be missed were I just to stop. I have been transformed by reading trans scholarship and by engaging with trans cultural production, affected precisely in the way that Susan Stryker predicted in 1994 when she wrote that "to apprehend a transgendered consciousness articulating itself . . . will remake you in the process" (250).[9] This change is personal, theoretical, and political, and it clarifies to me how feminist and queer discourse is not enough. Quite simply: writing from my position allows for the continued investigation of how feminism, including queer feminism, changes (and ought to change) in its encounter with trans thought.

From this standpoint, this text addresses an ongoing point of tension between trans and feminist politics, a tension that remains unresolved but that is especially apparent on the borderlands between "woman" and "nonbinary": is the "better" position to resignify womanhood (or, in my case, white womanhood in particular) or to refuse this social position? From what position is such a choice possible? Can this even be a "choice"? These questions return to key debates in the history of feminist theory. Played out in scholarly texts and on Instagram, they are at once new and old. They point to the ongoingness of problems never resolved, and, perhaps, never resolvable, but nonetheless still meaningful to many people both within and outside of the academy. Addressing them requires taking up Jane Elliott's call to challenge the common belief that "theory that is no longer novel is no longer useful" (2006, 1701). My central argument, that movement between "woman" and "nonbinary" is possible, insists that the oppositions that my central question depends upon needs not be synthesized. I can seek to recognize a nonbinary structure of feeling without giving up on the feminist project of resignification. Along the way, I can both inhabit and resignify "white woman" and also refuse the social position of "woman" though not necessarily the whiteness that is attached to it – here, only resignification is possible.

2.1 Nonbinary Genders and the Modern/Colonial Gender System

This thesis indexes how the analysis of nonbinary genders and the category "woman" needs to be developed within a historical context that understands how "gender," as María Lugones argues, is a "colonial concept" (2007, 186). What I mean by this is that gender is imbricated in the production of race and the nation, and the projects of colonialism and settler colonialism. For example, scholars in Indigenous studies, such as Joanne Baker and Mark Rifkin, have argued that binary gender (and its reliance on anatomical sex) is

---

[9] Attending to this transformation is also to follow Hale's rules for writing about trans-related material for people who are not trans (2009).

a colonial imposition, entangled with the imperial appropriation of land, bodies, and epistemologies. In this framework, the elaboration of Two-Spirit and other Indigenous genders and sexualities becomes a critical part of decolonization (Rifkin, 2010; McMullin, 2011; Barker, 2017, 13–15). In Black feminist studies, many scholars, such as Evelynn Hammonds (1997) and Beverly Guy-Sheftall, have traced how Black women have been "forever outside the ideology of womanhood" (Guy-Sheftall, 1990, 96). This is because the concept of "womanhood" as it emerged in the United States and Europe during the mid-nineteenth century was explicitly and implicitly white. My point here is an obvious one, though one that still remains difficult in some (mostly white) feminist scholarship: I cannot analyze the category "woman" without thinking of how that category has been imbricated in the production of race and racism, the projects of (settler) colonialism, and the nation.

From my positionality, I am especially interested in asking how white nonbinary positions relate to racialization. I ask this question not because I want to take attention away from Black, Indigenous, and people of color (BIPOC people) – although it is true that this attention can sometimes become another mode of surveilling control, a practice of othering, or a method to extract value (Gossett et al., 2017). Instead, I work in the tradition of whiteness studies that seeks to de-universalize whiteness by making whiteness visible as a historically constituted particularity entangled with dominance (Dyer, 1997; Alcoff, 2015; Rankine, 2020). Here, I ask, is the possible refusal of white womanhood also a refusal of whiteness? Or does even posing this question represent a white desire for continued, willfully blind, violent innocence?

Part of the challenge in addressing this question is that the privilege of whiteness often functions through hiding its existence as a particularity or as a category at all. For this reason, any claim to "escape" or "refuse" whiteness in fact seems to perform whiteness rather than to disrupt it. Such claims also seem to miss both the historical and present-day structures and daily interactions that constitute and reproduce whiteness. One cannot simply "escape" these through any act of volition, affiliation, or political solidarity. A second problem is that the category "white woman" signifies many different things both all at once and across time and space. For instance, it is (and has been) a demographic category; a structure of feeling and mode of affiliation; a category of self-identification; a violent ideal that lends itself to discipline, self-discipline, and exclusion; and, finally, a figure in public discourse, representative of those who hold a particular political stance, be that stance the Make America Great Again (MAGA) movement and/or colonial, nationalist enthusiasm for the mission of "civilization."

All of these modes of understanding "white woman" obviously overlap, and yet at the same time one can imagine the existence or presence of one without the other.

The collapse of these various positions was clear to me at the National Women's Studies Association (NWSA) conference I attended in November 2016, immediately after the election of Donald Trump. Conference attendees were reeling. Some people were surprised that many white women had voted for Trump, and during my panel's Q&A, white women in the room, myself included, were called upon to reach out to other white women to get them to change their allegiance. "But I am not a white woman," a white, senior colleague whose work is greatly admired in the field (including by me), insisted. Her argument went something like this: "My masculine gender performance means that even if I am white and a woman, I am not part of this category 'white woman.' That category has been defined against me. I'm not included." I wasn't so sure. While many white queer people understand their queerness as potentially or effectively deracializing, does not this understanding reproduce and depend upon racial privilege? "You are a white woman," I insisted to my senior colleague. "Your queerness is not relevant." But we were confusing things. Yes, demographically, she is a white woman, and yes, she might (or might not) practice modes of being, acting, and feeling that reproduce the habits of white womanhood, as a result of her socialization and structural position in this world. And yet at the same time, her sense and practice of affiliation as well as her politics need not align with the category.

The heated debate at the NWSA haunted me a few months later, as I attended an anti-racist workshop at my university. After several presentations, the organizers had us join discussion groups. These groups were mostly based in ethnic, national, and racial categories: Black, Asian American, American Indian and Indigenous, South Asian. There was also "white ally" and "white anti-racist." The final category, though, puzzled me: "queer and gender-nonconforming people." Presumably, the existence of this category suggested that queer and gender-nonconforming people have an orthogonal relationship to racial categories – that somehow gender and sexuality cut through racial, ethnic, and national belonging. It is of course true that homophobia, transphobia, cisnormativity, and heteronormativity exist, and that some of us lose (and then remake) our sense of kin as we come out, which might have the result of breaking our feeling of racial affiliation. It is also true that we live with the remains of late nineteenth-century white discourse, which used iconography associated with Black female sexuality to represent white lesbians (Gilman, 1985, 218). In this vision, sexual "deviance" was understood in the context of racial hierarchies and vice versa such that a white lesbian might be understood as not-quite-white.[10] And yet, certainly, at the same time, the space of queerness is and has itself been racialized – there are countless examples of how racism exists in these spaces even as some people contest it in these spaces too (see, for instance, Riggs, 1989; Puar, 2007; Hanhardt, 2013; Haritaworn and Riley Snorton, 2013; Marhoefer, 2022). Quite simply, white gender and sexual non-conformity can and do coexist easily alongside the maintenance of racial inequality and racial identity even if there is nothing inherent about this nonconformity that is itself racist.

In the sections that follow, the movement between "woman" and "nonbinary" that I focus on is a movement between the racialized position of white woman and another position that, I will explain, is also tied to whiteness, yet at the same time offers a potential for the transformation of whiteness too. In other words, there is nothing inherent to "nonbinary" that is anti-racist, although it could be anti-racist too. As Bobby Noble writes of white trans men: "That we transition into a masculine identity is not enough; we must also self-consciously and willfully embody an anti-racist, anti-White supremacist politic at the same time" (2006, 15). I will argue that a white nonbinary position does not offer a space of escape from race, but it does offer a potential or possibility for change. This is because the performance of "white womanhood" has often been reproduced for racist purposes, for the purpose of colonization. My point is not to conclude that the category "white woman" is unsalvageable or necessarily inherently racist. But I do risk asserting that it might be easier to develop a white nonbinary anti-racist position than one grounded in the category woman. "Nonbinary" potential disrupts the habits of whiteness, though not necessarily.

2.2 Toward a Politics of Care

Finally, my refusal of synthesis (between nonbinary and woman, between feminism and trans politics, between whiteness and its possible transformation) is based on an approach to politics that centers the practice of care over the purity of thought. I allow for contradictions that are apparent in the world. Instead of making an argument based on principle, I consider what it makes possible, who it might harm, and what it might allow.

Early feminist work in care ethics, notwithstanding its many limitations, is helpful in this regard. Without idealizing or naturalizing the mother–child relation and without falsely universalizing "woman's" experience, what I take as important from the legacy of feminist care ethics is its approach to moral questions. In the words of Nel Noddings, moral problems ought to be considered "not as intellectual problems to be solved by abstract reasoning but as

---

[10] Thank you to Laurie Marhoefer for helping me to articulate this point.

concrete human problems to be lived and to be solved in living" (1995, 23). The idea of universal moral principles depends upon "on a concept of 'sameness,'" one that is only possible in abstract (14). In the place of such sameness, Noddings allows for both difference and contextualization. Moral reasoning then ideally requires that actors "talk to the participants, to see their eyes and facial expressions, to size up the whole situation" (23).

My contention is that gender-critical feminism could use a return to the ethics of care, developing arguments that do not begin from abstract principles but rather from people's lives, developing arguments that are judged based on how fully they help people develop their projects, developing arguments that under-stand the enhancement of the quality of care in the world as a good. Central to the ethics of care is an attentiveness to the one cared for. In other words, the framework of care is not a cover for a paternalistic form of control. Care is not a "feeling for" others but a "feeling with" others (Hobart and Kneese, 2020, 2). We exist with others and are dependent upon them; it is for this reason that we are compelled to care, in fact. Because of our interdependence, "to care is to be sensitive to the constitutive otherness of both self and community" (Duclos and Criado, 2019, 160). That is to say, to care is not only to recognize possible differences between the self and the other but also within the self itself. Quite simply, feminist approaches to transness could benefit from this ethos, one that allows for difference between and within subjects.

Care also allows for a politics of contradiction. To argue that, in their encounter with trans thought, some feminists might evacuate the category "woman" might seem to continue in the tradition of queer and feminist theorizing that either implicitly or explicitly dismisses or even demonizes trans identifications with masculinity and femininity. However, I ask that we understand contradiction or tension not as a sign that thought is amiss but rather as a sign that the world is complex. In other words, I do not want to disagree with Vivian Namaste that "transsexuality is about the banality of buying some bread, of making photocop-ies, of getting your shoe fixed. It is not about challenging the binary sex/gender system, . . . it is not about starting the Gender Revolution" (2005, 20). But, at the same time, I do not want to give up challenging this binary either. We can seek a world where trans people can buy bread in peace; we can seek a world that does not discriminate on the basis of sex and gender; and, at the same time, we can work toward a world where sex and gender have proliferated. We can move between tense strains of thought, tense points of identification and not require that these positions be synthesized. We live with and in contradiction – our caring thought needs to be flexible enough to accommodate it.

Still more, centering care also has the potential to unsettle queer theory's attachment to antinormativity, an attachment that has sometimes been harmful as it has approached transness. As Robyn Wiegman and Elizabeth Wilson have traced, antinormativity is "a canonical belief in queer studies, if not its most respected critical attachment" (2015, 4). The field emerged in its analysis and critique of sexual and gender normativity, for instance, in the work of Judith Butler, Leo Bersani, Michael Warner, and Eve Kosofky Sedgwick. This antinormative sensibility, Wiegman and Wilson argue, is also central to the project of queer of color critique, for instance in the work of Roderick Ferguson (2003) and Jasbir Puar (2007), in as much as the field has understood heteronormativity as a racial project and homonormativity as an approach to queer politics that reproduces norms of gender, race, and class (Wiegman and Wilson, 2015, 8). But antinormativity has had important limits in trans worlds. For instance, in a foundational essay from 1998, Henry Rubin argues that the logics of antinormativity are often used to invalidate "the categories through which the [trans] subject makes sense of" their experience (265). For instance, Rubin looks to Bernice Hausman's argument (1995) that people who seek gender-affirming surgery recapitulate "gender normativity" (Rubin, 1998, 265). Although Hausman does not blame trans people for this, Rubin argues that Hausman's analysis misses any attentiveness to the lived experience of gender identity, the experience of "the people who inhabit transsexual subject positions" (265). This experience might not always seek to contest gender norms. Jay Prosser's *Second Skins*, from the same year, reads similarly. The text critiques the ways in which early queer studies, especially Judith Butler's *Gender Trouble* (1990), turned to transness as a figure for the instability of gender, sex, and sexuality. In contrast, Prosser asks, "what are the points at which the transsexual as transgendered subject is not queer?" (1998, 27). How might attention to the life writing and life experience of trans people trouble queer theory's destabilization of identity? Building on this work more than twenty years later, Andrea Long Chu and Emmett Harsin Drager argue that trans studies' understanding of the limits of antinormativity is precisely what it has to offer gender and sexuality studies: "The most powerful intervention scholars working in trans studies can make, at this juncture within the academy, is to defend the claim that transness requires that we understand, as we never have before, what it means to be attached to a norm – by desire, by habit, by survival" (2019, 108). The future of trans studies, Chu and Drager argue, "will be impossible with anti-normativity" (108).

   Chu and Drager's approach, as well as Rubin's and Prosser's, are motivated by a project of description – describing the attachment to a norm, describing the experience of being trans. We can understand this project of description as part of a project of care. To borrow from Joan Tronto and Berenice Fisher, such attention constitutes the first phase of care: "caring about, attentiveness"

(1995, 142). Interest in care has long been central to trans studies and trans politics, in fact. This is in part because for many (though certainly not all) people, being trans places them in a particular relationship to the health-care system: at times, seeking access to care and yet finding it limited for a myriad of reasons such as its long, continued history of racism, its practice of gatekeeping, its model of "transsexualism," its attachment to gender and sexual norms, and its entanglement in capitalist structures of exploitation (see Spade, 2006; O'Brien, 2013; Gill-Peterson, 2018a, 2018b; Malatino, 2020; shuster, 2021). Navigating these structures has often meant eschewing a politics of purity: Michelle O'Brien puts it this way: "We have to meet our needs, not through isolation, purity, or refusal, but through accessing and redefining care in ways counter to the institutions involved" (2013, 63). Care has also been central to the field because many trans subjects have been shut out from the traditional sites for the practice of care, notably, the space of the (heterocisnormative) family (Malatino, 2020). Within this context, developing alternative networks and spaces of care, or "care webs" in the words of Leah Lakshmi Piepzna-Samarasinha (2018), becomes critical to survival.

Highlighting the importance of care in trans studies and politics can help to reimagine queer studies. Antinormativity is not a good in and of itself – not even in queer studies. The attachment to antinormativity in queer and queer of color critique emerged as a part of a project of seeking to support the lives of those treated as expendable because they are or were seen as outside the boundaries of those worthy of care. Understanding antinormativity in this frame clarifies queer studies' important difference from neoliberal culture. Shannon Winnubst reads Butler's *Gender Trouble* as "a quintessentially neoliberal text" (2015, 125), one that celebrates nonconformity, which neoliberal culture itself champions as a "great value" (121). But neoliberalism champions nonconformity for the sake of innovation and entertainment. For Butler, it's a question of being, survival, flourishing – and this difference is crucial.

That said, it is true that "care" has functioned as a gloss for control, discipline, and biopower, a mode to "make live or let die" or to produce bodies that are economically productive and politically docile (Foucault, 1995). It is indeed true that many different kinds of projects can traffic in the language of "care." Michelle Murphy explains how "empire and capital can operate through acts of affection and care" (2015, 722), for instance in the myth of "white man's burden" (or white's women's burden), which legitimizes colonialism and settler colonialism, framing each as practices of care. One might read American Indian residential schools as one such project of settler colonial, violent "care." "Care" can also turn into "violent projects of conservation and defense" to protect those deemed unsafe from "the other" (Duclos and Criado, 2019, 159). It is in the name of such "care" that Texas governor Greg Abbott recently announced that offering gender-affirming care to transgender youth is a form of child abuse and ought to be reported to the Department of Family and Protective Services (Sharrow and Sederbaum, 2022).

Although "care" can and has been used in these ways, my tendency is to understand these examples as forms of care gone wrong rather than as a basis from which to question the value of care itself. That is to say, these are bad examples of care; they do not live up to the practice of care as an ethical ideal. Notably, they do not allow for difference between subjects or they frame that difference as a threat to the self. The first stage of care, a form of attentiveness to an other, is utterly missed in these instances. Within the contexts of our present neoliberal necroecologies, by which I mean, in a context of an ongoing pandemic, within the context of pervasive racial discrimination and disinvestment, in the context of ecological devastation and continued attachment to market logics to judge all worth, we need more care, better care, not less of it. Indeed, care consists in "a set of vital but underappreciated strategies for enduring precarious worlds" (Hobart and Kneese, 2020, 2).

The ethics of care guides my theoretical investigation, and if this text is successful, it will function as a practice of care. A work that cares for queer, feminist, and trans thought, which is to also say queer, feminist, and trans lives, a practice of maintaining, continuing, repairing, and also contributing to "our 'world' so that we can live in it as well as possible" (Tronto, 1995, 142).

2.3 Roadmap

The next section, framed as a response to Cameron Awkward-Rich's 2017 essay "Trans, Feminism: Or, Reading Like a Depressed Transsexual," develops a rebuttal to the claim that if someone has a particular bodily morphology, they must be female, and as a result, a woman. Drawing on trans phenomenology, as well as work by Sylvia Wynter (2003) and C. Riley Snorton (2017), I explain how the feminist insistence on the irreducibility and intractability of sex partakes in a logic that promotes the inequities of settler colonialism and anti-Black racism. As feminism encounters trans thought, a crucial space opens up for those of us assigned female at birth who have harbored a nonbinary structure of feeling. In this space, we can refuse the social position of "woman" (though not necessarily the whiteness attached to it) while also inhabiting and resignifying the position of woman as well.

Section 4 turns to a close reading of LiveJournal posts from the mid-2000s, tracing the development of "nonbinary" genders as they first emerged in the

English language. This section provides an ambivalent defense of nonbinary gender. It might be tempting to read "nonbinary" as a neoliberal containment of identity and its management (even branding), one that lacks the transformative power of queer politics. Along these lines, Kadji Amin understands nonbinary identity as a manifestation of the "liberal Western fantasy of self-determining, 'autological' selfhood," an ideal that stands in "opposition to the 'genealogical'" self, "overdetermined by social bonds, ascribed to racialized and Indigenous peoples" (2022, 116). Nonbinary identity emerges as part of the Western identity machine, Amin argues, and it is "therefore difficult to imagine an identity more provincially Western and less decolonial than contemporary nonbinary identity" (116). However, although it is true that nonbinary gender emerges within a white habitus, I show how the attachment to the term might also be understood as connected to a position that values care over nonnormativity, the maintenance of social bonds over the self-determining subject. Because of this, while nonbinary gender is certainly not inherently decolonial or anti-racist, it need not necessarily reproduce liberal and neoliberal selfhood either.

Section 5 argues that a nonbinary structure of feeling, one characterized by discomfort in white, female embodiment, can be found throughout Simone de Beauvoir's *The Second Sex* (1949). This discomfort need not be read as anti-feminist but rather as gesturing toward a desire for sexed transitivity that, at the same time, seeks to transform gender in its intersection with race, class, and religion. I turn to Beauvoir here because of her prominent position in the history of feminist philosophy and because this field, that is, the field of feminist philosophy, is currently an area of discursive production where we see the reproduction of anti-trans or gender-critical feminist thought (Irigaray, 1993b; Grosz, 2011; Stock, 2018; Allen et al., 2019; Lawford-Smith, forthcoming). Beauvoir's work has also been taken up in feminist discourse that insists on an intractability of the physical body (Rustin, 2020). To find both a nonbinary and feminist position in Beauvoir's texts is an attempt to intervene in this direction of feminist thought.

Overall, this text, written from an ethos of care, develops an anti-racist feminist, queer, and trans approach to nonbinary gender. Because I am writing from the positionality of someone who was assigned female at birth and who has inhabited woman, albeit uncomfortably, for some time, both the structure of feeling and identity of nonbinary that I consider throughout is one that emerges in relation to this past, and therefore in relation to "woman." But, just as not all women inhabit femininity in the same way, not all nonbinary people inhabit the category in the same way either. There are many women just as there are many nonbinary identities – this text is focused on one. I argue (1) that the assertion of nonbinary gender identity allows for a productive escape from patriarchal femininity (though not necessarily the whiteness that is attached to it), (2) that nonbinary gender need not be understood as necessarily reproductive of liberal and neoliberal selfhood, and finally, (3) that taking the example of Simone de Beauvoir, we can also understand nonbinary gender as a structure of feeling, one that can coexist with the desire to transform femininity and the social position of womanhood in its intersections with race, class, religion, and nation, as well.

3 "You Can't Not Be a Woman"

Cameron Awkward-Rich's beautiful work "Trans, Feminism: Or, Reading Like a Depressed Transsexual" (2017) provides an important model for thinking about the relationship between feminist and trans thought. The text is written from Awkward-Rich's perspective of trans masculinity. This is certainly not a limit of the text, but it calls for a loving response, from the other side, feminism. This section is that response. Starting with Awkward-Rich's framework, and recognizing that a disidentification with patriarchal femininity has been at the heart of feminism, I argue that the feminist encounter with trans thought opens the possibility for the feminist subject to refuse both femininity and the social category of "woman."

Feminism and trans thought, Awkward-Rich argues, offer "competing theories of gender that seem aimed at each other's annihilation" (836). For feminists – and here Awkward-Rich is speaking of lesbian feminists in particular, using Sheila Jeffreys as the primary example – "gender is an expression of power, never identity" (831). In this reading, transmasculinity is an effect of patriarchal misogyny, a "mismanaged" attempt to escape the pain of female, and especially lesbian, oppression (831). Awkward-Rich clarifies that Jeffreys does not represent all lesbian feminists, but her concern that transmasculinity displaces lesbian femininity and delimits the category "woman" has shaped much lesbian feminist and feminist discourse (Ginelle, 2014; Goldberg, 2014; Truitt, 2014). In contrast, for transmasculine thinkers, gender is more than a relation of power. Gender involves identity, as well as one's sense of belonging, felt sense and pleasure. In this model, while it is true that transmasculinity often consolidates itself in the displacement of the feminine, this need not mean that it partakes in or accepts the denigration of the feminine. Although feminist and transmasculine thought operate with different understandings of gender, Awkward-Rich suggests that both fields want each other, need each other (838). Feminism needs transness to de-essentialize the gender binary, while transmasculine thought needs feminism to critique the privilege and power of masculinity, to have, in shorthand, a "version of m/f" that does not reproduce "m>f" (838). Trans masculine thought also needs feminism for another reason: "because there is as of now no better discourse to describe the harm for failing to be f" (838–39). Awkward-Rich's essay is especially compelling because of its non-totalizing and grounded approach to theory. That is, Awkward-Rich allows for tension within the concept of gender itself, refusing the disciplinary impulse to seek resolution and coherence. Along the way, "Trans, Feminism" does not cover over the messiness of life and feeling for the purposes of thought. He writes, we may say, from the perspective of care.

That said, Awkward-Rich frames the relation between transmasculinity and this particular strand of feminism as symmetrical: both threaten one another, both need each other. This approach, as he himself acknowledges, treats feminism, and the example of Sheila Jeffreys' work in particular, with "generosity" (831). Awkward-Rich does this for two reasons. First, his method of reading, grounded in depression, incites him to "lean into worldviews that might be hostile" to his "very life" (831). He does not seek to resolve the bad feeling or pain that emerges in the encounter between feminist and transmasculine thought. Instead, reading like a depressed "transsexual," he sits in or with this feeling, recognizing the impossibility of closure, alongside, nonetheless, the possibility of something usable in the encounter. Second, he claims that arguments such as Jeffreys's continue to have purchase; they cannot simply be dismissed, but rather need to be understood so that we can "properly understand the appeal" (831).

However, it is worth highlighting how the harm caused by this version of feminism on trans people is not proportional to the effect of trans thought on feminists. For instance, most prominently, Janice Raymond's 1979 *The Transsexual Empire: The Making of the She-Male* has become a foundation to the argument that trans rights and recognition are an anathema to feminism. Raymond's work influenced the Reagan administration to curtail transgender and transsexual access to health care and government social services, and as Jos Truitt notes, such "exclusions have been directly linked to negative health outcomes and high suicide and mortality rates in the trans population" (Truitt, 2014; see also Stryker, 2017, 112). The claim that trans people harm feminists (and ciswomen) is misguided. For instance, as Charlotte Jones and Jen Slater explain (2020), gender-segregated bathrooms have become one focal point of debate, as gender-critical feminists argue that allowing trans women access to women's bathrooms is threatening – itself violent or leading to violence and sexual assault. Yet these "arguments are rarely based on empirical research"; trans people are far more likely to be assaulted in bathrooms than ciswomen (Jones and Slater, 2020, 847). As Sally Hines argues, "an emphasis on the link between the 'sexed' body and the identity and experience of 'woman,' not only continues to be reinstated in attempts to regulate the boundaries of feminism, but is routinely recalled to reinstate the trans body as the body of fear" (2019, 154). This leads to a practice of "embodied segregation and sex verification," to a feminism based on "purity" that, much like much right-wing populism, uses the language of "safety" and "common sense" to legitimize exclusion and violence (154).

My point here, simply, is to insist that the relationship between trans politics and this branch of feminism is not symmetrical. That said, Awkward-Rich is right when he contends that for Jeffreys, the recognition of trans people threatens her position as a feminist: "It's quite clear," he writes, "that for Jeffreys to recognize transmasculine discourse within her worldview would require her own annihilation as a feminist subject" (2017, 833). Whereas Awkward-Rich explicitly leans into his own depressive positionality, taking on the threat of annihilation to engage with Jeffreys, he does not, understandably, force this position onto Jeffreys. However, writing, so to speak, from the other side, I can, at least analogically. That is, replacing myself for Jeffreys based on our similarity as white feminist subjects, and adapting Awkward-Rich's framing, I want to read as a depressed feminist, leaning into the possibility of annihilation while accepting that resolution between transmasculinity and feminism may be impossible. As a feminist approaching the border of trans and feminist thought, I come to offer myself – and as a result, others around me – the possibility of not identifying or, more simply, not being a woman.

This chance is erased in Awkward-Rich's account, but it is a productive possibility that emerges in the continued encounter between trans and feminist thought. This is clear in Awkward-Rich's turn to the story of Peter Pan, for example. Awkward-Rich explains how several transmasculine thinkers have looked to boyhood as a way of figuring a "masculinity without phallic power" (834). Personified by Peter Pan, the boy becomes a feminist subject, yet, and this is Awkward-Rich's point, the boy is recuperated as the girl, or Wendy, is displaced: "female femininity is aligned with the static and decidedly unqueer time/space of adulthood" (835). Wendy loses her childhood and takes care of others as Peter Pan has all the fun. Awkward-Rich's goal is to figure a form of trans masculinity that does not displace Wendy, and he finds this balance, in the end, by arguing that the trans masculine and feminist subject need each other, even love each other, though that love may not always feel good. Awkward-Rich even turns here to Plato's *Symposium* (sung in the voice of Hedwig) to speculate that the two subjects may once have been one yet, split apart as two, now turn to one another, seeking, though never finding, lost wholeness. Over and again in his essay, we are presented with this twoness, "m" and "f," and these two positions, positions of social intelligibility, map onto ideological positions, too, trans and feminist. This twoness makes sense because Awkward-Rich is approaching the meeting of trans and feminist thought from the perspective of trans masculinity, and as he argues, "trans . . . despite protests to the contrary, is quite attached to a version of m/f (why else the insistence that you use 'my' pronoun to address me?)" (838). However, approaching this meeting from the other side, the attachment to m/f can be different. Awkward-Rich argues that feminism, especially queer feminism, turns to trans thought to develop the argument that there is "no predictable, and thereby no fixed, difference between m and f" (838). But (queer) feminism might want or even need something more: a possibility of social viability and embodiment that is not gendered or that is gendered differently, that does not fit "m" and "f."

Why, as Awkward-Rich takes for granted, does Wendy have to remain a woman? Who or what is telling her that she has to? Why does she stand in for female femininity? What are the power relations that make this position appear necessary? What if Wendy has never felt at home in her postpubescent body, femininity, and homosocial "women-centered" spaces? What if Wendy has consistently desired and built modes of relationality orthogonal to those structured by m and f? What if Wendy's primary connection to the category woman is the fact that she was assigned to that position at birth? And what if she feels relief at the possibility that she might become otherwise? Could Wendy not, in her encounter with trans masculinity, forge a place for herself that is not gendered or "nonbinary"? Could they not insist that they need not identify with masculinity as a precondition to inhabiting this place?

All of this, of course, raises more questions than answers. What do I mean by nonbinary? Can someone (who?) really just "choose" to become nonbinary or to identify as nonbinary? Shouldn't a disidentification with patriarchal femininity lead to a reframing of femininity that would accommodate a nonbinary structure of feeling rather than the rejection of femininity? And what is the place of racialization within all of this? How does the recognition that gender is racializing and racialized interrupt singular answers to these questions?

3.1 "She Has to Be a Woman Because She Is Female"

To begin, I consider the argument that Wendy needs to remain a woman because there is no possible alternative. Her body is female. There is no Wendy without this female form. She cannot will herself out of this through any form of identification or in response to any feeling because that feeling or identification is always taken from the embodied situation of femaleness. Following this train of thought, because Wendy is female, as an adult, she is also necessarily a woman. She might contest femininity but not the social position of woman-hood, based, as it is, on female embodiment. Related to this argument is an associated point: Wendy ought to be a woman not only because she is a woman but also because feminism requires her to be a woman. Without women, there is no feminism.

We see the expression of such arguments in many feminist texts, including, perhaps surprisingly, queer and trans feminist texts. To take just one example, I turn to Jack Halberstam's 2020 essay, "Nice Trannies." The arguments articulated in the essay imply that Wendy (whom, I should be clear, is standing in for me, while I am standing in for Jeffreys and "feminists") is necessarily female, and that this recognition is required for feminism.

Written in response to Andrea Long Chu and Emmett Harsin Drager's provocative dialogue, "After Trans Studies," but taking on Chu's work more broadly, Halberstam's essay, "Nice Trannies," challenges several of Chu's claims, including the argument that queer and trans studies ought to be clearly differentiated. Halberstam also addresses the central thesis of Chu's short book, *Females*, which posits that "everyone is female, and everyone hates it" (2019, 11). In this model, to be "female" is not to have a certain body, but rather a particular psyche wherein "the self is sacrificed to make room for the desires of another" (Chu, 2019, 11). In response to this claim, Halberstam makes one central point: "we have to face the truth about bodies. We are not all females, but we are all messy, incoherent, and fragmented, phallus or no phallus" (2020, 326). *Females*, Halberstam argues, is less concerned with making truthful arguments than in articulating a style or tone (326). In other words, the work is "bullshit of the finest order – persuasive, intuitively right on, and bearing no relation to actual bodies and experiences" (326). If we are all females, Halberstam insists, there "are no queer studies, no trans studies, no feminism. No lines can be drawn, no territory defended" (329). To say that we are all female does not allow us to critique heteropatriarchy, to name, map and critique misogyny and sexism. Feminism requires sex difference because feminism is a response to the world, a world where there has been inequality based on sex.

For the purposes of this argument, I do not take up Chu's work here. Instead, I focus on an element of Halberstam's response, the claim that "we have to face the truth about bodies" (2020, 326). This claim overlaps with Halberstam's point that "stone butches" (and here Halberstam gives Judith Butler, Leslie Feinberg, Valerie Solanas, and himself as examples) "are female people who hate being female but do not believe that any amount of nipping or tucking, packing or binding will change the way femaleness hurts when you are in it but not of it" (328). To be fair, in making this statement, Halberstam is not positing any universal principle against gender-affirming care or practices. As a characterization of stone butches, the claim is far more precise and not against these practices in toto. Halberstam's point, more specifically, is that these practices do not mitigate the pain of femaleness "when you are in it but not of it" (328). That said, reading Halberstam's statement about stone butches in combination with his argument that the truth about bodies must be faced, it is hard not to conclude that the text allows for female masculinity but maintains a fixed category "female" suturing that category to a particular corporeal form and arguing that feminism (and trans and queer studies) requires this suturing. In this model, gender transition is possible, clearly, but the transition across sex is, at best, improbable.

Halberstam's work has been controversial in trans studies, beginning with his early contention, in 1994, that "[w]e are all transsexuals ... and there are no transsexuals" (226). Vivian Namaste argues that Halberstam has developed a "discourse that is first and foremost about feminism and lesbian/gay politics" (2005, 20). This discourse does not "understand transsexuality on its own terms" (20). But even if we read Halberstam from the perspective of feminist and queer studies, his arguments do not quite hold. Halberstam's statement that "we" must face the truth about bodies suggests that Wendy, in a sense, is stuck. She will always be in, though she need not always be of, femaleness. Halberstam does not explain what it means to be "in but not of" femaleness. We might, however, understand the phrase in these terms: to be in femaleness is to be "in" a particular body, to be situated "within" femaleness. In contrast, to be "of" femaleness might be to see one's "acts, gestures, and desire" as emanating from or following from that situatedness (Butler, 1990, 136). But is anyone *of* femaleness? If the body is performative (and Halberstam's essay champions Butler's work), if we are starting from queer feminism, then "acts, gestures, and desires produce the effect of an internal core or substance" such that no one is "of femaleness," where that femaleness is figured as a "truthful" body, one that must be faced (Butler, 1990, 136). Being "of femaleness" is precisely the belief that this queer feminist vein of thinking has demystified.

Ironically, being "of femaleness" might make more sense if we are working from a trans studies framework. For instance, in "Phenomenology as Method in Trans Studies," Henry Rubin makes sense of his interviews with trans men, arguing that phenomenology provides a useful framework for analysis. Among the many important arguments that Rubin makes, he contends that "at the heart of transsexual desire" exists "the tension between the body image ... and the physical body" (1998, 274). Writing about one of his research subject's account, Rubin describes how Matt "knows his female body as it is for others but denies that his subjectivity equals the social interpretation of that female form" (276).

Rubin quotes Matt, who explains: "I never identified as a woman. I never identified with my body" (276). In this framework, one might be "in female-ness," in that this is a physical body that exists for others, but one might not be "of it," meaning that one does not identify with this body, that one develops a body image in tension with the physical body, and that one disidentifies with the prominent social interpretation of the female form.

In this reading, Wendy might be "in but not of" femaleness. But this does not mean, as Halberstam implies, that she is necessarily a "female person." My argument here is inspired by Bobby Noble's claim that female masculinity "works best when it marks spaces defined away from the conventionally defined female body as well as the male" (2006, 5). To take one of Halberstam's own examples, we can turn to Leslie Feinberg. I want to contend that it is not right to argue that Feinberg was a "female person," as Halberstam writes. Even though Feinberg understands hirself as transgender and not transsexual, hir writing does not frame hirself as a "female person." For instance, in *Trans Liberation: Beyond Pink or Blue*, Feinberg explicitly addresses a fictionalized interlocutor (or interrogator) who asks hir, "which sex are you?" (1998, 6). "It sounds so simple," Feinberg continues, "And I'd like to offer them a simple resolution. But merely answering woman or man will not bring relief to the questioner. As long as people try to bring me into focus using only those two lenses, I will always appear to be an enigma" (6–7). Feinberg does, however, go onto say that ze was "born female" (9); however, as ze comes to act in the world, this femaleness is accompanied by masculinity. That is, over and again in this text, Feinberg identifies as a "masculine female" (9) or as "a female who is more masculine than those prominently portrayed in mass culture" (7). To read Feinberg as a "female person" strips the masculinity without which ze does not appear in the world. It is to posit something that does not exist in the world, or that only exists as we turn hir body into an object, disregarding the body as it is lived.[11]

It is not surprising that trans history has many examples of stories where people's "true sex" is said to be revealed at death. It is the body as object not as lived perspective whose sex is extractable from gender. This body does not have the status of personhood. To take just one example, we can turn to the story of Murray Hall, which was written about in a 1901 article in *the New York Times*, "Murray Hall Fooled Many Shrewd Men."[12] The article claims that "the discovery of 'Murray Hall's' true sex was not made until she was cold in death." It is notable that it is in this sentence that Murray Hall's name is first

---

[11] This argument draws on Salamon (2010, 93).
[12] The article is archived in Katz (1976, 323–324).

placed in quotation marks. These quotation marks question his existence, suggesting that his personhood, indexed by his proper name, was not real. In other words, his "true sex" emerges as his personhood is withheld or deemed fraudulent.[13] Murray Hall is not a female person because his personhood was in question as he appears as female. It is only as a dead body and not a person that he is female.

This argument resonates with C. Riley Snorton's *Black on Both Sides*. Snorton argues that "sex" emerged as separate from gender within the violent context of transatlantic slavery. He turns to the case of J. Marion Sim's operations on three enslaved women – Anarcha, Betsey, and Lucy – operations that are central to the emergence of gynecology, and he argues that it is here that we find the emergence of the concept of sex. Operations on the enslaved people could be understood as producing knowledge that would be useful for the treatment of white women based on the argument that they shared a "sex." However, they did not share a gender, in as much as granting womanhood to the enslaved people would be to grant them, at a minimum, a shield from visibility. In other words, it is in the making of Black flesh as fungible and available to violation that we have the emergence of sex. Sex is not a natural condition of bodies so much as a violent product (2017, 17–54).

All this suggests that the "truth" about bodies that Halberstam would like us to face is a body stripped of subjectivity and personhood. Drawing on Sylvia Wynter's "Unsettling the Coloniality of Being/Power/Truth/Freedom," we might also argue that this body is consistent with the understanding of the human that develops as part of the coloniality of power, an understanding that, beginning in the mid-nineteenth century, describes the human "on the biocentric model of a natural organism" (2003, 267). In this model, Wynter argues, social and economic inequality becomes framed as the necessary outcome of evolution. Wynter explains: "the peoples of Black Africa . . ., together with all the colonized dark-skinned 'natives' of the world and the darker-skinned and poorer European peoples themselves, . . . find themselves/ourselves as discursively and institutionally imprisoned" (310). Social inequality becomes reframed as biological inequality, an inequity located in and explainable by the body as it engages in evolutionary competition. Wynter insists that unsettling the coloniality of power requires a new descriptive statement of the human, a new understanding of what it means to be human, drawing on perspectives that emerge from the ex-slave archipelago, such as work by Aime Césaire and Frantz Fanon. This understanding describes the human as a physiological story-maker.

---

[13] For more on Murray Hall, see Gearhardt (2019).

It is true that in this essay Wynter contends that unlike race, gender "has a biogenetically determined anatomical differential correlate onto which each culture's system of gendered oppositions can be anchored" (264). And yet, while anatomical difference exists, her work suggests that we need not understand this difference as determining – it is only determining of gender (or sex) in a biocentric model that sees biology as primary and misses the ways in which humans are also story-makers. The natural sciences, Wynter claims, "are . . . half-starved. They are half-starved because they remain incapable of giving us any knowledge of our uniquely human domain" (328). Along this line of thinking, then, I would go so far as to argue that the concept of sex as grounded in biology is part of coloniality of power because it is consistent with the descriptive statement of the human that is key to the expansion of colonialism and its inequality. Feminists should not be invested in this model.

All that to say: as a subject and a person, Wendy is not "stuck" as a woman or even "in femaleness" for that matter. While her body might have a certain form, that body as it is lived can transform, such that to insist on its necessary femaleness is to strip her of subjectivity, of feeling, and personhood (or performance, if you like) a stripping that might happen in the world but that feminist thought should not be invested in promoting, a stripping that is consistent with the description of the human as primarily a biological being, whose position in society can be explained by the biological sciences.

And yet, at the same time, that stripping does happen. As a result, if feminism is going to respond to the world, we do need to recognize that this happens all while contesting it at the same time. Wendy is not stuck in femaleness, but they might take the position on. They might note that they have been positioned, over and again, as a woman and see the limits of this positioning. They may want to transform what woman means socially and discursively. They might, in short, claim that their position need not be fixed: they can move between "woman" and "nonbinary" politically and affectively – though that movement might not always be recognized. None of this is to say that Wendy has a choice exactly either. Their social position depends on how they are recognized in the world, which itself is dependent, in part, on how they appear. In turn, their way of appearing depends on how we see, how we make sense of the world around us, and what modes of understanding are presented to us. This means that Wendy's position is not stable. It can change over time and in different contexts too. But the central point here is that Wendy might desire a position that is not gendered. She might not feel the possibility of pleasure within the category of "woman," even as it is remade. She might desire forms of relationality and belonging that are not structured by binary sex/gender. These feelings, this nonbinary structure of feeling, might call for something more than a queering of "woman." It might beg for a politics that asserts a nonbinary identity.

3.2 But Is Wendy Not Racialized?

So far in this analysis, Wendy has been deracialized, and she is in Awkward-Rich's essay too. Because of the way that whiteness functions as an unmarked supposed universal, one might argue that this deracialization is actually a racialization: Wendy appears here as implicitly white. In fact, in J. M. Barrie's original *Peter Pan*, Wendy is explicitly white: she plays the role of the civilizing mother to the lost boys of Never Land. The play, as Mary Brewer argues, is a "prime example of how dramatic representations of race helped to create and communicate a shared vision of what it meant to be a white British national as opposed to this subject's 'other'" (2007, 387–388). This history and context then raise the question: How has the argument that I have developed thus far been mediated or inflected by race? Is it Wendy's presumed whiteness that allows for her flexibility or movement across positionalities? In the section that follows, I analyze the development of nonbinary gender identities in LiveJournal posts on the FTM listserv from the early 2000s. Reading these posts, it is clear that the phrase "nonbinary" gender appears in a functionally white space, one interested both in changing public discourse and in seeking recognition. In other words, "nonbinary" emerges in a context of a politics of visibility, a project intent on seeking recognition. Visibility here is not understood as a tool for surveillance, control, judgment, and possible violence, so much as a pathway for intersubjective recognition (Decena, 2008; McCune, 2014; Snorton, 2014; Gossett et al., 2017). In this case, while "nonbinary" might be taken on as a move away from the category "woman," this movement is not a movement away from whiteness. The nonbinary position is just as white – or, more precisely, it is conditioned by whiteness, established within its habitus.

And yet, at the same time, this white nonbinary position allows for limited transformation as well. For Wendy, let us now substitute Amy Cooper, a white Canadian woman who, in 2020, called the police on Christian Cooper, a Black man bird-watching in New York City's Central Park. He had asked Amy Cooper to put her dog on leash, in accordance with the rules of the park. In response, Amy Cooper claimed to feel threatened, and called the police: "There is an African American man. He is recording me and threatening me," she repeated. In *Situation 11* (2020), a video about the incident that she made with John Lucas, Claudia Rankine acknowledges how, in calling the police, Amy Cooper shows her socialization into "repeated patterns of discrimination." She can "bet on racism, racial profiling, and possible unwarranted murder of a Black man." But Rankine does not read Amy Cooper's behavior as a performance of fear so much as of anger. Amy Cooper is incensed that a Black man might tell her what to do. She feels rage. This is a performance of possessiveness: the sense that property, public space, the world belongs to white people (Harris, 1993). It is an expression of rage that such possessiveness is not acknowledged by a Black man.

Rankine and Lucas's video presents Amy Cooper's actions as a familiar American story. It is the repetition of a long script, passed down across generations of white people. Amy Cooper's actions are an example of where the structural gets enacted through an individual who repeats sedimented habits and scripts. Cooper has been positioned to understand the world as her own and to produce the appearance of fear or tears when that possessiveness is not acknowledged.

Hers is a performance of whiteness, but of white femininity more specifically. As Rankine puts it, she "activates a covert white female power trigger that can easily call in the violence of white men." Amy Cooper "assumes her role as a piece of high value white property in jeopardy." White femininity's supposed innocence alongside its framing as a vulnerable yet valuable object of property to be protected and defended has the power to bring in violence with one swift phone call.

But what if Amy Cooper understood herself and was read, at least to some extent, as white and nonbinary? They would also be socialized into patterns of discrimination. They certainly could perform vulnerability too. They certainly could maintain the sense of white possessiveness. But they might less readily understand themselves as being able to call in the violence of white men, an ability in part structured by cisheterosexism. They might not necessarily understand themselves as "piece of high value white property." They might worry about how other white people might respond to them. Or maybe not. It is possible that in some more liberal milieus, they might see themselves as especially in need of protection and worthy of it. But given the unevenness of such frameworks, even in a place like New York City that might not always be the case. A blip might then enter into the sedimented habits and structures of the feeling of whiteness. There might even be a sense that because of their gender performance, the park is not in fact theirs – it is certainly clear to them that the country of the United States is not.

This is not to say that our fictional nonbinary A. Cooper would not then be white. Again, they will have been socialized into their position of whiteness. They will have benefited and benefit from the privileges of whiteness. And yet, the sedimented scripts of both white femininity and white masculinity would not readily be available to them. In other words: a central part of whiteness, especially as it is reproduced in habits and structures of feeling, is binary gender. This is not to say that white nonbinary genders will certainly not reproduce these habits and modes of feeling, but it is to say that such genders introduce some friction or tension into the inherited scripts. White nonbinary genders might reproduce possessive whiteness yet might less readily be given its violent riches. This might of course lead to heightened violence, the insistence that whiteness ought to be recognized. But it also might lead the other way, offering the possibility of an affective disalignment with the performance of whiteness and an inability and refusal to readily repeat its habits and scripts.

That said, not all Wendys, of course, are white. Moving from Rankine and Lucas's film, we can finally turn to the second episode of Terence Nance's 2018 television series, *Random Acts of Flyness*, which explores gender and gender relations in the Black diaspora.[14] The episode, much like this section and Awkward-Rich's essay, considers both feminist and trans thought together. Part of the episode revisits the story of Peter Pan, this time featuring a young Black man, Pan, who tries to convince a Black woman, Wendy, to become the queen or goddess of Nuncaland (*nunca* is Spanish for "never"). In this Nuncaland, boys do not grow up, and as a result, there are no men, no "Man." Nuncaland, in Pan's vision, is a world without patriarchy. But Wendy refuses Pan's offer. At first, she sings that she wants a man. "What kind of world would it be without men?" she asks. But as the scene progresses, she eventually comes to a different conclusion: "I want a human," she claims, "who will fight beside me."

In her encounter with the gender-nonconforming and nonphallic Pan, Wendy does not explicitly reject her gendered position. She is certainly not claiming anything about her identity either. However, in wanting a human who will fight beside her, she rejects two forms of sociality that the episode, ultimately, also rejects: both homosociality and heterosociality, both m and f. The episode is dismissive of lesbian feminism and also skeptical of the radical potential of masculine homosociality, including Black homosociality (as, for instance, upheld in Frantz Fanon's desire to be "a man among men" [(1952) 2008, 85] or Marlon Riggs's vision of the radical potential of Black men loving Black men [1989]). At the same time, the episode does not hide something akin to what Jane Ward might call the tragedy of heterosexuality (2020). That is to say, it offers no model of heterosexuality that is not harmful to Black women. Rejecting both homosociality and heterosexuality, rejecting both m and f, the

---

[14] Many thanks to Amber Jamilla Musser for bringing this episode to my attention.

episode posits something different: two humans standing beside one another, fighting together. These humans are not figured in a gendered relation so much as standing together in commonality. Both are growing older, the lyrics insist, and as adults, they take responsibility, in part to end patriarchy. This is, one might argue, a nonbinary structure of feeling in that it imagines a form of relationality not structured by binary gender and sex. It is true that the scene ends by repeating that Pan ought to take responsibility for his "father's faults." This phrase might seem to suggest that Pan ought to grow up and become a man, that we need men to displace patriarchy; it might seem to insist that only grown men can displace their fathers. But there is nothing in the lyrics or the visuals to suggest that Pan ought to become a man, necessarily. Instead, Wendy asks that they be human. In a word, the episode calls for a nonbinary Black feminism, one focused less on identity than on developing modes of relationality beyond binary sex and gender, modes of relationality focused, at least in part, on standing together to end patriarchy and white supremacy. This is the productive space that emerges in the encounter of feminist and trans thought.

4 The Online Development of Nonbinary Gender as a Practice of Care

The term "nonbinary" first emerged in the written English language during the mid-2000s, in online spaces, most especially on the social media platform LiveJournal and its community FTM blog, a largely white, middle-class, American space.[15] It appeared in an attempt to mitigate a central conflict on the FTM LiveJournal between those who sought to challenge, deconstruct, queer, or "fuck" "binary gender" and those who sought to inhabit masculinity. Whereas "genderqueer" became associated with the position that gender ought to be dismantled in toto, "nonbinary" became framed as a valid gender position, but one that does not seek to do away with gender altogether, and one that does not call transmasculine identifications into question either.

Here is what Eve K. Sedgwick might call the "paranoid reading" of the development of nonbinary gender on social media (2003): this development continues in the proliferation of identity categories, as this proliferation moves across sexology, psychology, and social media. This proliferation is about the management and containment of difference, one that fixes and categorizes (Foucault, 1990), one that imagines gender as psychic rather than social (Amin, 2022, 117). It values the promotion of difference for its own sake

---

[15] I focus on the emergence of the term "nonbinary" itself, but as the following chapter makes clear, I certainly am not claiming that there were no nonbinary genders prior to the emergence of this term.

(or at least for the purposes of marketing), treating differences as aesthetic positions, which is to say "preferences," as opposed to structural positions of power (Melamed, 2011; Hong, 2015). In addition, the emergence of nonbinary gender cannot be understood apart from the neoliberal valorization of the transparent, authentic self, the person who knows who they are, what they want, and actively goes after it (Clare, 2017). This form of personhood should not be understood as a sign of freedom so much as a description of neoliberalism's *homo oeconomicus*, the self-branded individual whose performance of transparency, self-sufficiency, and self-maximization facilitates capitalism (Foucault, 2008; W. Brown, 2015). Social media interpellates actors to become *homo oeconomicus*, and nonbinary gender is a by-product of that interpellation. Still more, nonbinary gender is attached to the racialized ideal of the self-determining subject, who is posited in distinction to the "genealogical subject overdetermined by social bonds, ascribed to racialized and Indigenous peoples" (Amin, 2022, 116). Related to this, we might argue that nonbinary gender emerges in a worldview that understands visibility and recognition as good in themselves rather than as traps or modes of surveillance and control (Foucault, 1995). Because of this, it is not surprising that it emerges in a white habitus (McCune, 2014; Snorton, 2014; S. Brown, 2015; cárdenas, 2016; cárdenas, 2017; Cho, 2017; Gossett et al., 2017). In a word, "nonbinary" is part and parcel of (neo)liberal, racialized platform capitalism (Melamed, 2011; Hong, 2015; Srnicek, 2016).

This section argues that while all of this might be true, it is also too simplistic, as it tells only part of the story. I contend that the turn to "nonbinary" might also be read as the manifestation of a political position that values care over nonnormativity, thus departing from the anti-normative impulse of queer thought. Nonbinary gender emerges within the contexts of functionally white trans, queer, feminist communities of care. These communities seek to develop useful narratives of the self in dialogue with specific others. The communities do not understand gender identity as self-determined or psychic, as opposed to social (c.f. Amin, 2022, 117). However, while gender is often figured as constructed as opposed to essential within these spaces, at the same time, the spaces support the habits and habitus of whiteness, as they are entangled with dominance. Although nonbinary gender does develop within a white habitus, it does not remain there and, in many cases, breaks from liberal possessive individualism as well.

To make this argument, I begin by tracing the emergence of the term "nonbinary" in online spaces in the early 2000s. I then develop an analysis of that emergence, focusing on the limited practice of care and the model of selfhood articulated and performed within these spaces.

4.1 From the Usenet to LiveJournal

Though certainly not uniformly or evenly, the term "nonbinary" has recently gained prominence over other related, possible words, such as "androgynous," "agender," "bigender," "genderfluid," and "genderqueer," to point to an existence that conforms neither to the position of woman nor man. None of these terms exactly map onto one another, and with the exception of "agender," the alternatives are all generally older than "nonbinary." They emerged at different moments in the history of trans, feminist, queer, and gender-nonconforming politics.

The use of the term "nonbinary" took off in the Anglo-American world in the 2010s, especially in the second half of the decade. The *Oxford English Dictionary* (OED) added the term in 2018, providing examples of its use mostly from the 2010s in the United States, Canada, and the United Kingdom. While the OED does include an entry from 1995 from USENET ("soc.support.transgendered"), this citation's use of the term stands out from the later ones because it frames "nonbinary" negatively (as something to emerge from into becoming a "real man or woman") rather than as a site of positive identification or inhabitation. The publication history of the term "nonbinary" aligns with the OED's account: several popular books were published about "nonbinary gender" beginning in the past few years (Barke and Iantaffi, 2019; Young, 2019; Vaid-Menon, 2020; Rajunov and Duane, 2021; Anderson, 2022). Before then, no books were published that focus on nonbinary genders, using the term. Unsurprisingly because of publication speed, media outlets featured "nonbinary" a few years earlier, and the term gained some prominence in 2014 when a petition to the White House gathered more than 47,000 signatures to recognize nonbinary gender.

To understand the emergence of nonbinary gender, however, one needs to go beyond print publications. That is, as the OED's first citation makes clear and as Avery Dame-Griff explains, online spaces have been central to the development of trans communities and vernaculars (2019, 2020). "The internet," Lal Zimman and Will Hayworth argue, "is a highly trans modality" (2020, 499): a place for trans people to connect across geographies and social circles, a place to interact "without the cultural baggage attached to our fleshy selves" (499). In fact, as Paul Byron clarifies, "digital trans communities, activism, and knowledge building is as old as the internet itself" (2021, 123). While these spaces have been central to the development of trans knowledge, support, and advocacy, they have also been the site of harassment and of endless spam. As many scholars have shown, "networked publics appear to reproduce many of the biases that exist in other publics – social inequalities, including social stratification around race, gender, sexuality, and age, are reproduced online" (boyd, 2011, 54). That said, these spaces can also be used to contest these inequities (e.g., see Bailey, 2021; Byron, 2021).

While the OED locates the first usage of the term "nonbinary" in the newsgroup soc.support.transgendered, the term was not in circulation in reference to gender at the time. During the 1990s, the Usenet was the primary location of online trans communities. There were five primary trans-related newsgroups: alt.transgendered, soc.support.transgendered, alt.support. crossdressing, alt.fashion.crossdressing, and alt.support.srs (Dame-Griff, 2019). On these newsgroups, the term "nonbinary" was widely used to reference images. That is, these newgroups were "nonbinary" groups, which in the parlance of the Usenet meant that people were not supposed to post images or "binaries" to them. There is much discussion in the newsgroups about this, and that I did not find any messages that play on a possible double meaning to the term "nonbinary" is significant: the word appeared often, but it was not used to refer to a gender position (or lack thereof).

Although "nonbinary" was not claimed in these newsgroups, the messages do include a sustained discussion about "binary gender" or the "two-gender system." During the first half of the 1990s, these conversations, which occurred almost exclusively on alt.transgendered, often drew on academic feminist theory and the emergent transgender discourse of the time (especially the work of Leslie Feinberg [1996, 1998] and Kate Bornstein [1994]). The posts index the influence of structuralism and poststructuralism, and especially deconstruction, on American queer, trans, and feminist thought. For instance, on June 3, 1993, Karen Fisher posted to alt.transgendered: "This culture is very caught up in dualities: male/female, light/dark, good/evil etc. Western philosophers have even on occasion stated that binary opposition is the **basis** of thought and language" (128159).[16] Her post goes on to reference Luce Irigaray and Monique Wittig and argues for the development of a "non-hierarchical language in which instead of thinking in terms of binary opposition, we think in terms of multiple differences" (128159). Many posters seem to agree with Fisher: dominant discourse treats gender as a binary but, as Joe Hary put it in a post on April 13, 1993, "gender identity is not 'binary.'" Hary went on to say that this critique of binary gender also tended to argue for the existence of a "continuum" or "spectrum" of genders (128326). In fact, during the first half

---

[16] In the pages that follow, I am citing from the Usenet, using the Transgender Usenet Archive, developed and maintained by Avery Dame-Griff, and accessible here: http://queerdigital.com/ tuarchive. I cite the posts with the message number, and I include the name of the person posting as long as the posts do not divulge what I consider personal information.

of the 1990s, so many people on alt.transgendered agreed with this point that on April 26, 1994, Heather Hansen posted: "It was others in alt.tg that . . . let me see for once and for all that gender is not binary."

Whereas people during the 1990s did not employ the term "nonbinary" to refer to someone's gender, the term is used in its contemporary sense on LiveJournal during the 2000s. LiveJournal is a social media platform that still exists (though it is now owned by a Russian corporation). In the United States, it was popular during the 2000s, especially during the first half of the decade before other social media platforms (such as Tumblr and Facebook) overtook it. LiveJournal hosts individual blogs and community blogs, which have their own webpage to which members can post. Lal Zimman and Will Hayworth (2020) claim that it is on LiveJournal, starting around 2007, that the term "nonbinary" took over "genderqueer" and "genderfuck" as the most popular word to describe gender identities beyond man and woman. Their work develops a quantitative analysis of this transition, counting the use of actual words over time in the four most active trans LiveJournal communities: FTM, transgender, genderqueer, and MTF. Zimman and Hayworth show that, similar to the development of other trans-related linguistic variation, the term "nonbinary" first became most prominent on the FTM LiveJournal and then got taken up in other trans communities on LiveJournal. "Socially powerful groups," they argue, "exert control over linguistic norms and, specifically, the meaning and acceptable usage of words" (512). This, they claim, can explain why the linguistic transformation appears on the FTM LiveJournal first: "transfeminine people consistently face more, more intense, and more violent types of transphobia than do transmasculine individuals" (512).

More can be said, however, about this change in linguistic norms and the location of this change. First, building on Zimman and Hayworth's argument, it is also worth noting that the FTM LiveJournal was a functionally white space. What I mean by this is that the posts rarely (if ever) considered the intersections of racial and gender-based oppression: the focus was on gender as a separate axis of experience. This means that in order to participate, BIPOC people would feel pressured to overlook racism and white privilege and because of this, it seems fair to argue that the white habitus of FTM is connected to dominance. There were three other prominent intersectional trans and queer LiveJournal spaces at the time: TRANS_POC, IN_THE_LIFE, and QUEERPOC, communities that Zimman and Hayworth do not analyze. That said, when I read through these LiveJournal blogs, I never once found the term "nonbinary." Instead, it emerges within the white habitus.

That habitus is also connected to institutions of higher education. More specifically, the term "nonbinary," at least in written language, appears to emerge from among a group of people connected to institutions of higher education. For instance, consider the two earliest written uses of "nonbinary" on LiveJournal: on March 28, 2001, toby explained that they went to a campus "gender outlaw discussion group," which had them realize that even though they had "rejected the gender binary (at least in theory) for years," they felt that they needed "to be on one side or the other, or at least working toward one. . . . Welcome to the world of non-traditional, non-linear, non-static, nonbinary gender!" they wrote. The other instance is from September 17, 2002, when Eli Green posted a call for papers to several LiveJournal communities, including FTM: "Are you transgender, transsexual, genderqueer, gender bending, partner of a nonbinary gendered person, or a trans-activist? I am interested in incorporating your thoughts and words into a book that I am writing / editing." Green posted from a university email address and explains that the goal of his book is to contribute "a greater understanding to trans identity, foster discussion, and expand the very small amount of academic literature on the trans topics." Both of these early posts suggest that "nonbinary" emerged in multimodal contexts (across discussion groups, online spaces, and published works), contexts that were connected to higher education. The term "nonbinary" seems to reference the earlier conversation about "binary gender" on the Usenet. It points to the long influence of structuralism and poststructuralism on Anglophone thought.

In addition, reading through the take-up of the term "nonbinary" on LiveJournal, it is also clear that the term emerges within the context of a central conflict on the FTM LiveJournal between those who seek to challenge, deconstruct, queer, or "fuck" "binary gender" and those who seek to inhabit one of its two positions. This is especially clear in a January 27, 2003, post that received many replies. Given that I think it is important, I reproduce the post, written by Dj dannyboi, in its entirety:

My latest thoughts on the binary: there seem to be opposing camps out there. Binary vs. nonbinary. However, I think even the nonbinary are not all the same. For instance, I don't like the binary. But I don't want to expunge it from existence. I just want to have another option or four. Heh. But really, I don't understand how it has become such an us versus them kind of discussion. Every time someone posts something that includes the topic, they either say something like, "I know I'm gonna get shit for this," or someone will comment with, "This will probably piss people off but I think you have some good points."

I know we are all obviously interested in our own particular trans status. But I just can't quite grasp the reasons for the divide along these lines. The last drawn out discussion about genderqueers shed some real light on what people were thinking when they heard the term "genderqueer." I was really better able to understand where some of the anger was coming from. And really it had nothing to do with who I consider to be in the category of GQ. And I think some others got some understanding about the broadness of that particular category.

I guess what I really wonder is: for those people who don't see any problem with the binary, do you see someone like me as a woman? Do you think I should just pick one of the two choices? I am not asking these questions with any sort of animus really. Just pure curiosity and a desire to understand. Or is your desire to keep the binary more in opposition to the people who want to abolish the whole thing altogether and not have M or F or anything else?

I read this post as implicitly arguing for a movement away from the language of "genderqueer" toward "nonbinary." Dj dannyboi recognizes how, especially for those who seek to and do inhabit the position of a man, "genderqueer" has become a term to which anger has become attached. Whereas "genderqueer" is associated with the position that gender ought to be dismantled in toto, in this post, Dj dannyboi offers "nonbinary" as merely a valid gender position (even if "the nonbinary are not all the same"). "Nonbinary" does not do away with gender and does not seek to call transmasculine or transfeminine identifications into question, either, but asks for more options than two.

A similar argument can be made in response to many posts on LiveJournal. To take just one more example, consider Icarus_after's November 27, 2005, contribution:

i am male identified. i think of myself primarily as a man, not as a trans person or any other identity built around my history or my body. i also largely think of myself as post transition. however, i was strongly identified as "bi gendered" or, for lack of a less loaded term, "genderqueer" up to the time i began testosterone, and i know what it is to live as a visibly gender variant adult.

. . .

there may be a misconception that i am anti "genderqueer;" that is not true. while i am less and less able to understand nonbinary identities, i am not in a position to judge the places other people find comfort. i am not, however, comfortable with genderqueer+ identities being lauded at the cost of male and post transition identities being disrespected. i was surprised to learn in my own transition just how different the experiences of medically transitioning men are from the experiences of nontransitioning men/women/butches/ people who are female bodied and trans IDed, and i think there needs to be room for that to be acknowledged without coming across as one-upsmanship.

In this post, "genderqueer" is a "loaded term" that is sometimes "lauded at the cost of male and post transition identities being disrespected." While Icarus_after claims that he cannot always "understand nonbinary identities," he seeks to grant the existence or validity of this position. Again, then, "nonbinary" emerges in this post within a space of conflict, and its eventual preference over "genderqueer" seems to signal an attempt to mitigate tension, to move away from having to choose one position as more valid than the other.

Compare this post, for instance, to that of Chubbyfemme, who, on June 9, 2004, posted to FTM about a new LiveJournal she was starting, GENDERPIRATES: "i've created this community as an attempt for all gender-fuckers to meet each other, share information, rant, and help each other destroy the binary gender system. Everyone regardless of identity welcome. This includes non-trans people and femmes of course!" GENDERPIRATES did not get widely taken up. It only has a few posts to it. But reading this announce-ment alongside Dj dannyboi's, we can note an obvious difference in tone. While it is true that Dj dannyboi's call for more than two possibilities can be read as an attempt to destroy the binary gender system (more than two is hardly "binary"), at the same time the post recognizes how "genderfucking" or "genderqueer" may threaten some trans people's desire to inhabit a normative gender position. In contrast, "nonbinary" is less about a critique of normativity than about wanting the recognition of something else equally valid. The choice of the term "nonbinary" as opposed to "genderfucking," "genderqueer," and "gender-pirates" highlights the difference in intent: the latter words literally embrace nonnormativity and explicitly frame themselves as disregarding propriety, convention, and law (given the connection to pirates). In addition, in contrast to "nonbinary," "genderfucking" and "genderqueer" can be read as verbs: both are positions that do something to gender, either fucking it or queering it. "Genderpirates" might not be a verb, but it likewise suggests an action: pirating gender, taking it illicitly, robbing it. Quite simply, "genderqueer" is framed in the anti-normative style of queer theory and politics.[17]

In contrast, nonbinary, at least as it emerges on LiveJournal, departs from genderqueer's anti-normative attachments. It does not want to destroy gender and is offered as an attempt to mitigate conflict. Does this mean that the move from "genderqueer" to "nonbinary" is a politically quietist one? A retreat from the more in-your-face style of queer politics? Is the development of nonbinary gender on social media a sign that it is symptomatic of the containment, compulsory transparency, and self-branding of identity typical of social media? How are we to understand the term's emergence in a functionally white space, connected to higher education? Is there something inherently white about it? Having traced the emergence of nonbinary gender on LiveJournal, I now turn to an analysis of that emergence.

---

[17] The term "genderqueer" is often credited to the political activist and writer Riki Wilchins, who also claims to have coined the term in relation to queer theory (2017).

4.2 "Nonbinary" and the Limited Practice of Care

It is possible to read the emergence of nonbinary gender as a symptom of (neo) liberal, racialized, platform capitalism. For example, the category is clearly provincial, in that it emerges among a group of relatively privileged, mostly white people who are connected to spaces of higher education and who carry over the language of structuralism and poststructuralism. Next, the term also appears attached to the project of defining identity categories and seeking that these categories be visible and recognizable. The thought that we should come up with another gender position (or perhaps lack thereof) suggests that people should know who they are and be transparent about that – a practice that is especially valued on social media (and also valuable for the purposes of marketing). Indeed, many of the posts that discuss nonbinary gender are focused on identity: they seek to understand how to figure the self in public. We might even argue, following Amin, that the category "nonbinary" posits a self-determining subject, a formation that is racialized.

However, while none of this is exactly wrong, it does not hold onto the fundamental tensions or contradictions embedded in the emergence of the term. Most centrally, it does not consider how nonbinary gender emerged within communities of care: communities that sought to invent and create usable language for the self in dialogue with others. As Hil Malatino explains, "For far too long, both hegemonic and resistant cultural imaginaries of care have depended on a heterocisnormative investment in the family as the primary locus of care" (2020, 6). In addition, "the feminist literature on care labor and care ethics are steeped in forms of domesticity and intimacy that are both White and Eurocentered, grounded in the colonial/modern gender system" (7). Trans care requires a different theory and practice (see also Marvin, 2019). That said, the difficulty in this analysis is the fundamental ambivalence of the FTM LiveJournal site. On the one hand, I do want to argue that the site was a community of care and that recognizing this means that the mode of selfhood it imagined and reproduced with the idea of nonbinary gender is not simply neoliberal or liberal. On the other hand, I also want to recognize that this community centered relatively privileged, white subjects in a way that contributed to the marginalization of trans BIPOC people.

Holding both of these statements at play, I begin by describing FTM as a care network, a place where subjects went both to provide and to receive care, such as advice and support. FTM was a site for what Malatino calls the "infrapolitical ethics of care": "the forms of care that enable co-constituted, interdependent subjects to repair, rebuild, and cultivate resilience in the midst of, and in the aftermath of, experiences of overwhelming negative affect" (43). In the case of

FTM, a large part of this work involved "intimate storytelling" where people (in this case, especially white people) would tell their stories and construct a sense of self in a community different from the potentially isolated, hetero-, cisnormative social networks they had access to in real life (IRL) (De Ridder and Van Bauwel, 2015). The LiveJournals were also sites to share information and to develop alliances and relationships that could translate into advocacy. These platforms could offer support from invested, anonymous peers, forms of support that both recognize "a diversity of experiences and that nobody is an expert" (Byron, 2021, 137). They offered "experiences of identity, belonging, and ideological affiliation," and they helped "to make the management of everyday life possible" (Cavalcante, 2016, 118).

Although there was disagreement on the FTM LiveJournal, the journal's profile insisted on a practice of care: "you can come to this community for support, advice, information about Trans-related topics, questions about gender, personal connections with other FTMs, and anything else FTM-related that you can think of." This ethos is also reflected in its list of community rules and its profile's recognition that FTM is a "blanket term" covering "people with a wide range of identities and at many different stages of transition." As a result, the moderators ask that participants "refrain from making assumptions or judgments about people's identities and backgrounds" and be "open-minded and respectful" even in the face of disagreement. Overall, the ethos here is to prioritize the practice of care over the practice of being right. This ethos is carried over in the development of the term "nonbinary" over "genderqueer." The goal is not to theoretically debate gender so much as to support the lives of those marginalized because of nonnormative gender embodiments. The term becomes popular not in an attempt to fix difference and proliferate categories so much as in an attempt to make space for gender difference for the sake of well-being, respect, and (faux-universal/functionally white) community.

The analysis of social media, however, cannot simply be based on the discussion of the posts themselves but also of the platform(s) on which they appear. As José Van Dijck explains, "different sites' architecture cultivates distinct styles of connectedness, self-presentation, and taste performance" (2013, 34). This is another reason the paranoid reading is too simplistic: it does not consider the differences between social media platforms. Because of the specific features of LiveJournal in the early 2000s, it is too simplistic to argue that nonbinary gender emerges as part of the culture of neoliberal, platform capitalism and its valorization of the transparent, branded self. Existing scholarship on queer and trans social media practices has often focused on Tumblr, a microblogging platform that was especially popular between 2009 and 2015 (Bailey, 2021, 47; Byron, 2021, 147). Before Tumblr, however, there was LiveJournal, and LiveJournal shares some of the features of Tumblr. First, in contrast to Facebook and similarly to Tumblr, the community blogs were content driven, and not personality driven. When a user posted to the community blog, viewers could see their LiveJournal name, but the platform brought more attention to the post itself, which would be much larger than anything else. Next, like Tumblr, LiveJournal did not insist on users having one profile or presenting an authentic, transparent self. Instead, as the names of the authors of the posts I have cited so far make clear, users could experiment with and construct multiple avatars. This allowed people to join communities with less concern about who might see them. It also meant that the site's architecture, at least at its start, was less amenable to profit. In fact, although LiveJournal now shows advertisements on its community blogs, in its early days, it did not. Because of these features of LiveJournal, it is not fair to say that nonbinary gender is part and parcel of platform capitalism's neoliberal *homo oeconomicus*. The ethos here is not about promoting the self but rather on developing community. In fact, to be able to ask for and receive care requires unlearning "the shame that has become attached to asking for help, offering, and accepting help when we've been full-body soaked and steeped in the mythos of neoliberal, entrepreneurial self-making" (Malatino, 2020, 2).

Finally, the development of nonbinary gender on LiveJournal does not assume that gender identities are predefined, fixed, or singular. In making this argument, I am drawing on Mel Chen's analysis of Asian FTM transition-related YouTube videos (2017). Chen argues that the videos constitute a usable archive, not "moribund repositories" but "generative resources for identity" (157). The videos assume that "identities are not preset. They are live, constructed, presentist, futurist, real" (157). Something akin to this is present in the LiveJournal community blog. There seems to be an ethos of figuring things out, of change. We see this, for instance, in Icarus_after's November 27, 2005, post. He does not claim that he *is* male, so much as male identified. He writes about how he thinks of himself, and he recognizes how his self-identification has changed over time. He also claims that while he thinks of himself as a man, he also knows what it is "to live as a visibly gender-variant adult." In other words, he may have a political identity as trans or gender variant alongside a male gender identity. None of this is a language of stability or fixity. It doesn't exactly hold onto a notion of the authentic self as it recognizes that identification is a practice, an act: he is "male identified." Icarus_after offers "nonbinary" as what Chen might call a "generative resource for identity" (157). These identities are both real and constructed, in part with others. They might change in the future too.

Imogen Binnie's novel, *Nevada* (2013), which features a white transfeminine blogger, Maria, from the early 2000s, also attests to this ethos on LiveJournal. Binnie figures the practice of blogging akin to the confessional or to talk therapy, but with some important differences:

> The Internet at that time was this big, exciting place where you could anonymously spill your guts about gender and discomfort and heteronormativity and how weird male privilege felt and lots of other things, except back then she [Maria] didn't really have language for it so she just went like: everything sucks and I am totally sad. Just over and over and over and over . . . .. It couldn't have been very compelling to read, but writing about it at length made her pay attention to patterns and stuff and introduced her to the first real-life trans people she met, even if they were on the Internet. . . . She'd stay up all night, night after night, gushing her feelings all over the Internet until she figured out she was trans, transitioned, and wound up having the exact same problems as every other messed up . . . person in New York. She doesn't post there as much as she used to but she still has that blog. People read it. . . . It's kind of nice although . . . sometimes being the big sister is exhausting. (59)

This description chronicles how online spaces became forums for meeting trans people. They were sites of pedagogy and the intergenerational transmission of knowledge, even places for the formation of kinship (Binnie writes that Maria sees herself as a big sister). While it might be tempting to read these online spaces in concert with Michel Foucault's critique of the confessional, a central mechanism of disciplinary control that seeks to fix identity, I read this passage as also opening toward a less constraining mechanism, one that Chloé Taylor (2005) helps us to understand as a practice of the self, a form of hupomnênata. Drawing on Foucault's late writing on the self (1988), Taylor argues that such practices often use writing not to reveal "a true or pre-existing self," but rather to partake in the "always unfinished constitution of a self through citation and reasoned thought" (Taylor, 2005, 64). Amy Shields Dobson, Brady Robards, and Nicholas Carah, citing Eva Illouz, make a similar point in their discussion of therapeutic language on social media: this language, they write, "is not merely a ploy to discipline subjects and pathologize those unable to conform, but is a *resource* that is good for 'addressing the volatile nature of selfhood and of social relationships in late modernity'" (2018, 12; Illouz, 2007, 71). Likewise, in this passage, Maria is figured as using the practice of writing, to and with others, to create a social place for herself. That creation or production is not offered as a coming to terms with the self within preexisting logics but, rather, as developing language or creating new positions. Critically, while Binnie writes that Maria "figured out she was trans" and that she "transitioned," the place that she winds up is not figured as stable, either in this passage or in the novel. Maria has "exact same problems as every other messed up ... person in New York," and she eventually takes a road trip, leaving New York, though arriving, in the end, nowhere. The subject remains in flux, still looking for relationships and language to make life more livable.[18]

In short, I understand the development of nonbinary gender on LiveJournal as structured by a series of tensions. While the development of the term is clearly an example of the proliferation of identity categories and can be seen as symptomatic of the continued valorization of identity and the authentic, transparent self (the person who announces themselves as "nonbinary"), it also emerges as part of a practice of care. That practice does not fix gender identity so much as allow for transformation (even growth), eschewing notions of fixed gender identities and seeking to forge selves, to make something collectively that is both constructed and real. In this view, the self is constructed with and dependent on others. Next, while the emergence of the term "nonbinary" does posit a self-determining subject who announces their own gender, that subject is not sovereign. By this, I mean to say that the FTM LiveJournal was a site where people went to forge connections, to create socialities, to build the self with others. Nonbinary gender emerges within a space that recognizes how we need others – we need to be cared for, we need to be with others who care about the same things as we do, we need forms of sociality that can support our flourishing. So the nonbinary subject is only self-determining *with others*. And finally, "nonbinary" appears as a way to bring together trans-identified people across their gender differences (though not racial difference). It is not about being right about the nature of gender so much as about making a space for mutual support. In this way, "nonbinary" seems attached to a politics of care (for particular others) over a politics of antinormativity. Because nonbinary emerged as part of a practice of care, I do not see the term's emergence and eventual preference over "genderqueer" as a move away from politics but rather as a reframing of politics toward care work, a practice of fostering the relationships and acts that are "necessary for survival and flourishing" (Malatino, 2020, 45).

And yet, this practice of care clearly centers subjects who are relatively privileged: the FTM LiveJournal was a functionally white space that especially centered people with access to higher education. In this way, while the category did not necessarily posit essential gender positions, it certainly did emerge

---

[18] I have turned to *Nevada* here out of hesitation to cite from the LiveJournals. While I do cite the discussions about genderqueer and nonbinary identity, I have decided not to cite the more personal posts that seek for or offer guidance and/or support. *Nevada*, in contrast, is an explicitly public work in relation to which the ethics of citation do not seem as hazy.

alongside the continued fixity (which is to say reproduction or maintenance) of the racial habits of whiteness. The self that it seeks to develop with others seems content to build itself within a community that takes racial privilege and dominance for granted, or at the very least, a self that is comfortable with bracketing these questions. This highlights a danger of a politics of care: often, it is easier to care for subjects that are proximate to or somehow similar to the self. A politics of care must be attentive to who is receiving the care, or on what conditions. "Trans care," as Malatino argues, "can all too easily reproduce hierarchies of attention, aid, and deservingness and that such hierarchies exacerbate and amplify inequities. Any care praxis worth enacting must be attentive to such tendencies to reproduce injustice" (69).

Although nonbinary gender first appears within a white habitus online, it certainly does not remain there. Tumblr was started in 2007 and quickly became the preferred trans and queer social media platform in the United States. As Moya Bailey explains, "Queer and trans people of color (QTPOC) were a thriving component of Tumblr community and are responsible in large part for bringing 'trigger' and 'content' warnings in to the mainstream consciousness, along with the more notorious practice of the 'callout,' alongside its more gregarious sibling, 'calling in'" (2021, 147). It is also in this online space that we see a wide take-up of the term "nonbinary." As part of her chapter on the digital resistance of Black women and Black nonbinary, agender, and gender-variant folk on Tumblr, Bailey interviews Antoinette Luna Myers, a producer of important material on Tumblr for Black women and Black people. Drawing on her interview, Bailey explains that both in Myers's "corner of the web they carved out" on Tumblr and in their "elite liberal arts school setting," Myers was able to develop a "gender fluid identity" as "nonbinary," an identity that they were "really comfortable" with. That said, Myers does not "dislike being read as a Black woman," as is often the case in her day-to-day life. Bailey explains Myers understands "Black woman" as "one facet of a prism through which they still experience love and recognition. 'Black woman' does not encapsulate all of her, but is still a part of her that she understands that other people may recognize. 'Black nonbinary femme' is yet another facet of the prism through which she can be seen and recognized" (168–69). In this framework, the proliferation of identity categories such as "nonbinary" or even "nonbinary femme" should not be understood as an attempt to fix the self or to present a transparent, branded subject either. This is also not the identity categories of surveillance or disciplinary control. The model refuses the possessive individualism connected to white liberalism, too, where the individual is a "moral whole" and free to the extent that "he" is "the proprietor of his own person" (Macpherson, 1962, 3). Instead, these passages highlight how one's positionality depends on how one is "seen and recognized" (Bailey, 2021, 168). This indexes a lens that frames the self in its relationships with others. Nonbinary offers a place to move, to breathe, and to become with others. It is constructed, which certainly does not make it any less valid, and it emerges, at least in part, in an online space of care.

5 Beauvoir's Nonbinary Structure of Feeling

On first glance, it appears quite obvious: Simone de Beauvoir was not nonbinary. The category was hardly an option for her in twentieth-century France. That aside, and perhaps more importantly, it seems a stretch to argue that Beauvoir showed signs of a nonbinary structure of feeling in her writing. For example, the introduction to *The Second Sex* states quite clearly: "If I want to define myself, I first have to say, 'I am a woman'; all other assertions will arise from this basic truth" (2011, 5). Beauvoir also insists that "no woman can claim without bad faith to be situated beyond her sex" (4). Likewise, in her *Memoirs of a Dutiful Daughter*, Beauvoir explains that as a child, she "felt no disappointment at being a girl" (1974, 55). Describing her feelings as a postpubescent young woman, she again makes the same point: "I certainly didn't regret being a woman; on the contrary it afforded me great satisfaction" (295). The book's original French title, *Mémoires d'une jeune fille rangée* (1958), suggests that the young girl is properly ordered, tidy, even put away (this is what it means to be *rangée*). But the title also makes it appear that it is girl who is being well-arranged or positioned, not that she is a child being positioned as a girl. Quite simply: it is clear that Beauvoir figures herself as always having identified as a woman or a girl, and not being upset about this.

Reading more closely, however, things quickly become more complex. For instance, when Beauvoir explains in her memoir that she "felt no disappointment at being a girl" (1974, 55), she then elaborates: "As I have already said, I did not lose myself in vain desires but happily accepted whatever was given" (55). In this sentence, Beauvoir shifts from the *I* of the biographer, who has already said something, to the *I* of the child, who did not "lose" herself "in vain desires" (55). The juxtaposition of these two *I*s suggests that it is not just the *I* as a girl who "accepted whatever was given" but also that the *I* of the biographer would understand wishing something else as "vain." The choice of the word "vain" (which is the same in French) here is interesting. The desire is vain as in it is judged to be worthless, or useless – in other words, having the desire would lead only to frustration. But "vanity" also suggests indulging in one's own appearance. The sentence then points to precisely some of the themes we see in discourse that is disparaging of transness: first, that transition is impossible; and second, that a desire to transition constitutes an excessive attachment to one's appearance. The passage reads as though Beauvoir did not feel disappointment because such disappointment would be vain – not because she was not potentially disappointed. Reading the passage raises the question: If the desire were not judged as vain, would it then emerge?

This section argues that a nonbinary structure of feeling infuses Beauvoir's writing, especially *The Second Sex* and *Memoirs of a Dutiful Daughter*. I focus on this autobiographical text in particular because it describes Beauvoir's experience of puberty, which is to say an experience of becoming increasingly sexed, and one that the memoirist has memory of, unlike the experience of being sexed at birth. Too often, feminist readers of Beauvoir have dismissed her as being overly attached to masculinist values and norms. This attachment, it is said, is especially evident in her negative descriptions of the female body (Lloyd, 1984; Moi, 1986; Okely, 1986; Léon, 1988; Woodward, 1988; Hekman, 1990; Irigaray, 1993a; Grosz, 1994; Kristeva, 1995). More recently, claiming to "rescue" Beauvoir, some feminist philosophers have argued that Beauvoir does make a space for the valuation of a new femininity and the specificity of female embodiment, especially in her description of eroticism (Bergoffen, 2003; Heinämaa, 2003; Moi, 2008). Against these two readings, I argue that a nonbinary structure of feeling, one characterized by discomfort in white, female embodiment and a longing for a nonsexually differentiated form of human embodiment, can be found in Beauvoir's writing. This discomfort need not be read as antifeminist but rather as gesturing toward a desire for sexed transitivity one that, at the same time, seeks to transform gender. That is to say, the authorial voice that emerges across *The Second Sex* and *Memoirs of a Dutiful Daughter* develops both a feminist and trans position, a dual position whose feelings in the world, both past and present, too often have been dismissed.

This section is divided in three subsections. I begin by outlining my reading method and explaining what I mean by a "nonbinary structure of feeling." Having laid this groundwork, I then address a particular debate in feminist scholarship concerning *The Second Sex*, focusing on responses to the text's descriptions of embodiment. This debate is significant because of the ways in which it leaves no possibility for a nonbinary structure of feeling. Finally, reading *The Second Sex* in dialogue with *Memoirs of Dutiful Daughter*, the last subsection focuses on both texts' descriptions of the experience of female embodiment, descriptions that the memoir makes clear are not experiences of femininity tout court, but of white, bourgeois Catholic femininity more specifically. Moving between analyses of Beauvoir's texts and my own experience, I show how the situatedness of Beauvoir's account need not be read simply as the internalization of masculinism. Instead, the writing gestures toward a desire for an inhabitation of the body beyond binary sex, an inhabitation that does not flee from facticity but desires to transform that facticity. Beauvoir's nonbinary structure of feeling interrupts the scripting of her body into the reproductive imperative of the French nation-state and its "civilization." Attending to this structure of feeling is not to claim that femininity and masculinity – in their intersections with race, class, and religion – ought not to be transformed but to allow that Beauvoir's structure of feeling would not find resolution in the remaking of the feminine, either, for this is not the only content of its longing.

5.1 Reading for Structures of Feeling

In contrast to anything that we might read as trans or nonbinary in her writing, readers of Beauvoir do not have to interpret far beyond the surface to find lesbian or queer sexual desire. In fact, an entire chapter of *The Second Sex* is dedicated to the lesbian (417–36), and Beauvoir transitions to the chapter by arguing that "there subsists in many women . . . a tendency toward homosexuality" (416). *Memoirs of a Dutiful Daughter* is less explicit, but it is in paying attention to its passages about lesbian or queer erotic desire that we can develop a method of reading, a method with which we might then identify a nonbinary structure of feeling in Beauvoir's writing as well.

In the memoir, Beauvoir describes how she loved her best friend, Élisabeth Lacoin, known as Zaza, and was "completely won over by Zaza's vivacity and independence of spirit" (1974, 94). Beauvoir explains that she did not really consider the nature of her love: "I had been brought up to equate appearances with reality; I had not learned to examine what was concealed behind conventions of speech and action" (94). This passage intimates that while Beauvoir as a child did not understand her love for Zaza as sexual, Beauvoir as biographer thinks that her emotion went beyond convention. Another passage reads similarly. Here, Beauvoir recounts her interest in Marguerite de Théricourt: "I had no wish to be an intimate friend of hers; I simply wanted to be able to gaze upon her from a little nearer at hand. When I reached the age of puberty, this feeling grew stronger" (103). Beauvoir recollects taking an exam during which she was preoccupied with Marguerite: "I was too ignorant and too respectful to allow myself even the slightest stirring of desire; I could not even imagine a human hand ever profaning those white shoulders; but all through the examination I couldn't take my eyes away from her and I felt a strange tightening of my throat" (103). In this section, too, Beauvoir purports that as a girl, she did not allow her feelings to take the form of sexual desire, and yet, at the same time, there is something queer here, a "strange" feeling in her throat. Beauvoir's interest in Marguerite intimates of a queer potentiality, a feeling that is only ever emergent.

I read these passages as instructive. That is, they demonstrate that sometimes one can have feelings for which one has no name. These feelings index tendencies and potentialities, moments of possibility that, if articulated or allowed, could become more elaborate if not altogether different. The feelings point toward something without necessarily being that toward which they point. For example, they might be suggestive of trauma even if they themselves are not articulated and organized by the term "trauma." As Linda Alcoff puts it in a searing critique of both Michel Foucault and poststructuralist feminism (and especially Joan Scott's "The Evidence of Experience"), "experience sometimes exceeds language; it is at times inarticulate" (2000, 256). Such inarticulate experience is still meaningful, however. Alcoff gives the examples of date rape and marital rape. Before we had these concepts, such rapes still happened, even if they were not understood as rape. Likewise, before a child has the concept of sexual abuse, a child who is abused will likely find the experience traumatizing. Alcoff's point is that sometimes we feel in ways that we cannot put into language. Because of this, feminist theorists, she argues, ought to attend to bodily experience not as "endpoints or data that require theoretical illumination, but as capable of shedding light on theory itself" (269). This in fact has been a central project of feminism, Alcoff insists: to understand old experiences differently, to attend to experience as a basis for creating language that alters past, present, and future experience along the way.

In *Memoirs of a Dutiful Daughter*, Beauvoir herself recognizes that she sometimes had feelings that she would not allow herself to narrate or to develop. These were, one might say, nascent feelings. Convention shaped her understanding of feelings and even her very feelings themselves even as those feelings intimated toward the existence of something beyond convention. I am following Beauvoir, then, in allowing at least for the possibility that her writing points to possible trans feelings even if the philosopher does not name them as such. This reading method is especially convincing because of the way that Beauvoir portrays herself in *Memoirs of a Dutiful Daughter*. She is dutiful, a "good girl," doing what is expected of her. Beauvoir understands herself as hard working, studious, and ambitious but as somewhat conventional, notwithstanding her desire to become a successful writer. It would not be surprising if Beauvoir as an adult writing *Memoirs of a Dutiful Daughter* would continue, along the path of her childhood, to show signs of nascent feelings that point to somewhere else than where the text explicitly develops.

The ethics of this approach might be questionable, of course. It is one thing for Beauvoir-the-memoirist to return to her memories of girlhood and suggest that something was there though not acknowledged: queer or lesbian desire. It is another altogether for me as reader to go back and find something else.

This reading practice departs from what appears to be a basic principle of contemporary trans politics: as Talia Mae Bettcher argues, "Trans politics ought to proceed with the principle that transpeople have first-person authority (FPA) over their own gender" (2009, 98). To Bettcher's argument, one might add all people. If Beauvoir writes that she was and is a woman, I certainly cannot and should not challenge that. But I do not want to make an argument that Beauvoir was actually trans. Rather, I argue that a nonbinary structure of feeling can be found in her writing. I want to separate these feelings from a particular identity.

To think of nonbinary structures of feeling as opposed to nonbinary identities is helpful in this context for several reasons. First, this approach allows me to recognize repeated patterns of feelings, affects, even impulses and tones. I can read these patterns as nonbinary without categorizing the feeling subject in an identity category, without even insisting that "nonbinary" is an identity category, which has the property of something articulated and instantiated. This means that nonbinary structures of feeling can be present alongside normative gender identifications. It means that I can read for the presence of nonbinariness not as a position in itself but as an affective modality in relation to existing positions. Related to this point, understanding nonbinary as a structure of feeling means that I can recognize the presence of something even as modes of thought and worldviews have understood them in different terms. This allows for a reading method that embraces what some might understand as ahistorical. I look across historical periods and bring attention to the resonances between an authorial voice of the past and a reader, myself, in the present. Still more, approaching nonbinary as a structure of feeling underlines its sociality: sure, such structures of feeling are often "taken to be private, idiosyncratic, and even isolating," but they are shared modalities of feeling that develop in response to the world. This sociality of structures of feeling is one of the reasons José Esteban Muñoz draws on Williams too: emotion, he writes, arises in the "active negotiation of people within their social and historical matrix" (2020, 12). In other words, structures of feeling are socially contingent and relational. Finally, reading for nonbinary structures of feeling encourages us to recognize the existence of repeated feelings themselves as meaningful.

It is true that to interpret the impulses, tone, and affects in Beauvoir's writing as a nonbinary structure of feeling is to take feeling and place it in the realm of the articulated. It is to articulate those feelings within a particular worldview or ideology: I am interpreting in relation to feminism but also and more centrally in response to trans studies and trans politics. I want to argue, however, that to read the feelings as nonbinary is to take them at their word, not to dismiss them as false consciousness, for instance. My "surface reading" (Marcus and Best, 2009) sees them for what they are: discomfort and nonidentification with binary sex, especially as it has been elaborated in white, bourgeois, Catholic culture and desire for a nonsexually differentiated form of embodiment.

My reading of Beauvoir builds on recent work by Megan Burke and A. Alexander Antonopoulos, both of whom find some degree of trans potentiality in *The Second Sex*. Antonopoulos goes so far as to read the text's chapter on biology as a "transmasculine manifesto," arguing that the chapter describes the "biopolitical production of woman" but imagines a form of living beyond that production, a "somatic and corporeal potential" that would ultimately "contradict the biological 'truth of sex' and its production of the given" (2017, 474). Antonopoulos's reading is certainly provocative, and I will draw on some of his arguments in my interpretation, but manifestos are public declarations that seek to clearly promote a position, and transness does not appear in this register in *The Second Sex*. In turn, Burke rereads the calls to fraternity in the conclusion of *The Second Sex*, recognizing how they have been interpreted as signs of Beauvoir's masculinism and her renunciation of the feminine (2019, 3–4). In the place of these readings, Burke argues that Beauvoir both "affirms sexual difference *and* commits to an androgynous future" (4). As Burke insists, "Beauvoir's conception of sexual difference does not refer to mere anatomy, but considers the way difference is constituted through the entanglement of biological, affective and sociopolitical dimensions of our existence" (11). If that is the case, then affect in part constitutes sexual difference and a first-person claim to genderlessness is not the same as women's inauthentic flight from femininity: Beauvoir "encourages women to pursue freedom as women. Yet this may not be an authentic choice for everyone" (2020, 102). Burke's central point is that genderlessness or androgyny are ethically and politically sound positions in *The Second Sex*. My argument goes further than Burke's, though I also draw on her reading. It is not only that Beauvoir allows for the potential of androgyny, it is also that a nonbinary structure of feeling can be found in Beauvoir's writing and might even be said to motivate the writing, as well.

5.2 Feminist Approaches to *The Second Sex*

This nonbinary structure of feeling is especially apparent in Beauvoir's descriptions of the female reproductive body, passages that are notorious and well known. For instance, in her chapter on biology in *The Second Sex*, Beauvoir describes puberty as a process wherein the "species reasserts its rights" over a woman (39). She writes that when a woman menstruates, "she feels most acutely that her body is an alienated opaque thing" (41). Cramps are symptoms of the "species . . . eating away at" women, a "hostile element . . . locked inside them" (42). Pregnancy, too, is presented as a condition of alienation (36), a process that requires the "abdication" of "individuality" (36) and "demands serious sacrifices" (42). "Childbirth itself is painful; it is dangerous" (42). Breastfeeding is just a bit better: "exhausting servitude" (42). Overall, Beauvoir argues that it is for the "purposes of reproduction" that a species becomes sexually differentiated (21), and that the human female experiences that sexual differentiation as a negation of her selfhood such that "woman *is* her body as man *is* his, but her body is something other than her" (41).

How are we to read these passages? Do Beauvoir's descriptions suggest that human female embodiment is inherently lacking, such that feminism is doomed to fail? Is Beauvoir merely describing the experience of human female embodiment within patriarchy? Indeed, the chapter on biology ends by underlining how "physiology cannot ground values: rather, biological data take on those values the existent confers on them" (47). In other words, to use the language of existentialism, there is no essence that precedes existence; instead, one's existence is the basis from which meaning can be developed. Because of this, as Beauvoir argues, biological facts do not have "meaning in themselves" (46). Instead, first, Beauvoir draws attention to the influence of cultural and religious norms: "It is not as a body but as a body subjected to taboos and laws that the subject gains consciousness" (47). Next, she highlights the importance of social and economic structures, contending that we cannot consider "in abstract the burden of the generative function for woman. . . . [I]n humanity individual 'possibilities' depend on the economic and social situation" (46). And finally, Beauvoir insists that "biology" is not fixed either: the body does not form a "fixed destiny" for woman, "woman is not a fixed reality but a becoming," and "nature only has reality . . . as it is taken on by . . . action" (46). Overall, in the tradition of existential phenomenology, Beauvoir concludes that our bodies consist in our situation in the world, but these bodies are situated and therefore are not stable, either. They are lived bodies, not objects.

However, even if we contextualize Beauvoir's descriptions of female embodiment in this way, Beauvoir's descriptions are often read as going too far. For example, while Beauvoir recognizes the situatedness of embodiment, she insists that "woman's enslavement to the species is tighter or looser depending on how many births the society demands" (46).[19] This sentence suggests that no matter what, female reproduction is a condition of subjection.

---

[19] I am repeating Constance Borde and Sheila Malovany-Chevallier's translation here, but the French original term is *asservissement* (Beauvoir, 1949, 75), which can mean "enslavement" but also "subjection," a less loaded term that suggests Beauvoir is not necessarily, though certainly possibly, being myopic to the politics of slavery.

As a result, as Judith Thurman puts it in her introduction to the 2011 English-language translation of *The Second Sex*, "many readers have … been alienated by Beauvoir's visceral horror of fertility – the 'curse' of reproduction – and her desire, as they see it, to homogenize the human race" (xv).

Indeed, it is easy to understand Beauvoir's descriptions of female embodiment as a result of her upbringing. Beauvoir was raised in a Catholic, white, patriarchal French family that understood itself as elite even if it was not always rich. This somewhat precarious status was dependent upon a particular inhabitation or performance of femininity. Many passages of *Memoirs of a Dutiful Daughter* make this clear. "In our universe," Beauvoir writes, "the flesh had no right to exist" (1974, 58). The body was seen as indecent or inherently sinful, and a "lady," which is to say a particular racialized and classed woman, must respond to this body by covering it over, containing it in order to maintain the status of the racialized class (82). Reading *The Second Sex* next to *Memoirs of a Dutiful Daughter* clearly suggests that the descriptions of embodiment found in *The Second Sex* are influenced by this racialized, classed, and religious framing of female embodiment. In this view, Beauvoir never quite broke from the culture in which she was raised. Rather, she internalized its perspective.

Arguing along such lines, but in a more philosophical as opposed to an autobiographical register, Genevieve Lloyd argues that masculinism is present within Beauvoir's own philosophy, especially in "her remarks about female biology" (1984, 99). Lloyd's influential *The Man of Reason* contends that the issue is not that Beauvoir is describing the female body as it has been constituted in "'the present state of education and custom,'" as Beauvoir herself claims (quoted in 1984, 100). Beauvoir, Lloyd argues, is not simply describing the experience of the female body as it has been constituted by patriarchal culture. Instead, she is relying on the concept of transcendence, which is itself masculinist: in the philosophical tradition that Beauvoir draws upon (as elaborated in work by both Hegel and Sartre), transcendence has been conceptualized as the "transcendence of the feminine" (1984, 101). For this reason, women's pursuit of transcendence implies the transcendence of their femininity and, Lloyd implicitly contends, the acceptance that the female body is somehow lacking (because to value transcendence is to deem femininity and the female as that which ought to be overcome). In making this argument, Lloyd asks several rhetorical questions that remained unanswered, at least explicitly: "Can objectification of consciousness make one's very body other to oneself? Why should a woman's direct experience of her own body be an experience of lack of transcendence, or immersion in life?" (99). Ultimately, Lloyd implies that Beauvoir has overly internalized patriarchy, taking its objectification and denigration of the female body as her own experience. This argument suggests that even in patriarchal culture, another experience of the female body is possible. One might go so far as to conjecture that Lloyd herself experiences her own body in different terms, such that when Lloyd reads Beauvoir's argument that during menstruation, "a woman feels her body most painfully as an obscure, alien thing," Lloyd herself does not identify with that feeling, or, at the very least, if she does, then she also harbors the desire for a different feeling, too, and perhaps feels self-recrimination to the extent that that feeling does not materialize.

My movement here to the personal may appear inappropriate if not fallacious. I do not mean to deny either Lloyd or Beauvoir a philosophical voice, but I understand their philosophical voices as at least partially informed by their experience. Although *The Second Sex* is far from a memoir, Beauvoir is sometimes explicitly, and other times implicitly, writing about her own experience. Lloyd is too, as am I.[20]

When I first encountered Lloyd as an undergraduate, I loved *The Man of Reason*. It helped me to understand my own situation – especially in my math classes at the time – and it helped me to give voice to cultural norms I had noticed but could not quite articulate. And yet at the same time, also as a first-year undergraduate, reading Beauvoir's descriptions of experiences of the female body offered me great relief. *Beauvoir understood how it is that I felt.* Before reading her, I felt alone. After that first semester, I was hooked on feminist thought, and I have been immersed in it for over twenty years, and yet I still identify with some of Beauvoir's descriptions of the experience of the female body. For this reason, and as I will elaborate, I cannot simply dismiss Beauvoir as overly attached to patriarchal culture; I cannot simply read these descriptions as her internalization of the Catholic, white bourgeois culture in which she was raised. Something resonates in Beauvoir's writing about female embodiment: an impulse or affective pattern, one that is not at all pre-social, even if it is experienced as individualizing, but one that develops in response to and as part of the social world. It cannot just be that Beauvoir and I are bad feminists, or that we are or were especially susceptible to internalizing norms and attitudes that do not serve us. There is something more (or perhaps something less, which is not to say lesser, but more primary, more superficial): a structure of feeling is at play.

It was also as an undergraduate (this time, second year), that I first encountered Irigaray's philosophy of sexual difference. I was assigned *Je, tu, nous: Pour une culture de la différence* (I, You, Us: For a Culture of Difference)

---

[20] This reading method is similar to Kathleen Woodward's approach to Beauvoir in "Rereading Simone de Beauvoir's *The Coming of Age*" (2018) and her earlier "Simone de Beauvoir: Aging and its Discontents" (1988).

(1992). The book begins by addressing *The Second Sex*. Irigaray recognizes that it was a groundbreaking and influential text. Yet Irigaray registers its (and Beauvoir's) limits. She recounts how while she herself sought out Beauvoir's support as a feminist "sister," Beauvoir did not respond after Irigaray sent her a version of *Speculum, De L'autre femme*. "Why?" Irigaray asks. Was the gap between them merely generational? Yes, to some extent, but Beauvoir did work alongside younger feminists (8). Did it have to do with Irigaray's attachment to psychoanalysis? Yes, in part, that too: both Beauvoir and Sartre (Irigaray notably adds here) were resistant toward psychoanalysis (9). But ultimately, Irigaray suggests (at least implicitly) that the problem was Beauvoir's masculinism. The reason Beauvoir did not respond is not only that she was not interested in sexual difference but also, and more centrally, that to the extent that she had not cultivated a culture of sexual difference, she did not value relationships between women, mothers and daughters, and feminists. Irigaray explains how, in contrast, her psychoanalytic training encouraged her to develop a different approach to feminism than Beauvoir. Whereas Beauvoir, Irigaray contends, seeks equality, Irigaray, as is well known, seeks a culture of sexual difference. Equality, Irigaray argues, re-centers men: to be equal is to be equal to men and to assume the values of patriarchy. The framework of equality does not account for how the human species is divided into two genders (*genres*) and how this division allows for both production and reproduction (10). So long as feminism does not recognize the centrality of this division, feminists risk working toward the destruction of women and the destruction, Irigaray goes so far to argue, of all values. Irigaray uses strong terms here: wanting to suppress sexual difference, she claims, is to call for a genocide more radical than any other destruction in history (10). We have yet to develop a culture that accounts for sexual difference; instead, we've had a culture of sexual sameness, a culture of masculinism that features the feminine as a negation or lack and not a positive difference in its own right. That positive difference might be elaborated in myth, language, and also in writing about the female body, as Irigaray makes clear, for instance, in "When Our Lips Speak Together" (1980). In Irigaray's view, because we have not developed this culture of sexual difference, we are currently in the "infancy of culture" (*l'enfance de la culture*).

In the connections that Irigaray draws between the development of culture and sexual difference, one hears echoes of the argument that sexual differentiation is a sign of civilization's racial progress. But as an undergraduate, I will be honest to say that this is not what rubbed me the wrong way. Nor was it the supposed essentialism of Irigaray either – which was a central topic of debate at the time. My response was more affective than reasoned. This positive femininity that Irigaray imagined – I could not imagine myself in it even as

I understood that it did not yet exist – I didn't want it, though I could not exactly say why. I preferred the space of negation; the space that was undefined, the not or the non.

"Why subject yourself to her?" Judith Butler finally asks in seeming exhaustion as they discuss the work of Irigaray in conversation with my own (beloved) dissertation advisor, Elizabeth (Liz) Grosz, as well as Drucilla Cornell and Pheng Cheah (Cheah et al., 1998). Long before I read this interview, I had decided not to take Liz's class on Irigaray, though I loved Liz's lectures and learned plenty from her. But I couldn't bear to read more Irigaray. In Butler's question, and the affective drive behind it, I see my own aversion, even as Liz's response makes sense too: Irigaray's work has been central to feminist philosophy in part because of the power of her arguments concerning sexual difference. In her work, sexual difference is a condition of life itself, and a concern for ontology, ethics, politics, linguistics, religion, aesthetics, and so on. When I was told in a reading group on phenomenology, this time as a graduate student, that we should not read Beauvoir because her work was sociological and not properly philosophical, I turned to Irigaray to fight the claim.

Irigaray has also been central to a later group of readers of Beauvoir, claiming that while Beauvoir did offer negative descriptions of the female body (especially in her descriptions of the body as a bioscientific object), at the same time, in parts of *The Second Sex,* one can find positive valuations of sexual difference that refuse to judge the feminine body-subject according to androcentric values (Bergoffen, 2003; Gatens, 2003; Heinämaa, 2003; Moi, 2008). Sara Heinämaa, for example, argues that Beauvoir "rejects the assumption of sameness. Women and men are not opposites, she argues, but neither are they identical" (2003, 82). This is especially evident in Beauvoir's writing on female eroticism, Heinämaa claims, and it points to how Beauvoir thinks "in terms of difference" (82). Debra B. Bergoffen makes an overlapping argument, contending that *The Second Sex* speaks in two voices (2003). The first voice insists that women ought to make themselves subjects just like man – developing projects, refusing bad faith, and engaging in transcendence. This argument, according to Bergoffen, supports the logic of the one. But another, albeit muted voice, a voice that advocates for sexual difference (or the logic of the two), is also present in *The Second Sex.* This difference is apparent in Beauvoir's insistence that the human is always sexed, in her attention to embodiment and the lived situation, and in her writing on heterosexual bonds and the erotic (Bergoffen, 2003, 249).

These are convincing readings, but they accept that negative descriptions of the experience of female embodiment in *The Second Sex* are either a sign of masculinism or something that ought to be explained away or surpassed. They also continually return to a binary structure of thought where one is either male or female, man or woman. And while this is a valid reading of *The Second Sex*, others are possible. Beauvoir, I want to claim, has been both misunderstood by those who accuse her of masculinism and those who have sought to reread her work to find the positive valuation of sexual difference within it. Neither of these readings, I want to contend are exactly wrong, but both miss what I read as a central affective impulse in the text.

5.3 A Nonbinary Structure of Feeling

Reading for structures of feeling, we can recognize how the authorial voice that develops across *The Second Sex* and *Memoirs of a Dutiful Daughter* is characterized by a nonbinary structure of feeling: a disidentification with the female sexed body, a desire for a form of embodiment that has not been differentiated for the purposes of reproduction, and identification with aspects of both traditional masculinity and femininity.[21]

To develop this argument, I begin by bracketing the question of ontogeny. Lloyd asks, why would a woman experience her body as something other to her? This is a reasonable question within the context that Lloyd poses it, and Lloyd's implicit answer is that this experience is the result of a woman taking on a masculinist point of view. Read in a trans and queer context, however, the question becomes less transparent. In *Epistemology of the Closet*, Eve Kosofsky Sedgwick refuses what she calls the question of ontogeny, "What is the cause of homo- [or of hetero-] sexuality in the individual?" (1990, 40). This question, she argues, has been developed "from the essentially gay-genocidal nexuses of thought" (40). She continues: "my fear is that there currently exists no framework in which to ask about the origin or development of individual gay identity that is not already structured by an implicit, trans-individual Western project or fantasy of eradicating that identity" (41). Instead, "gay-affirmative work does well when it aims to minimize its reliance on any particular account of the original of sexual preference and identity in individuals" (41). Following Sedgwick, it seems more than reasonable to suggest that currently there exists no framework in which to ask about the origin or development of a trans identity or feeling that is not already a project of eradicating it. Lloyd's question, why would a woman experience her body as something other to her, can be rewritten as a question about why someone might feel that their body is other to

---

[21] I use the term "disidentification" simply as the opposite of "identification." I do not, however, mean it in the ways that it has been developed by Muñoz (1999). I use the term as opposed to, perhaps, "lack of identification" or de-identification. I neither want to understand this feeling as a lack – this framing suggests that something else ought to be there, and I also do not think "de-identification" is right, for it suggests undoing something that was first present. The prefix "de" usually means to undo, whereas "dis" reverses the action of the verb it precedes.

themselves. This feeling might then be understood as an expression of gender dysphoria. Lloyd's argument seeks to eradicate the feeling by changing the subject's point of view. In contrast, rather than posing the question of ontogeny, I want to draw attention to the feeling itself. In other words, I invite us to pause in our reading of *The Second Sex*. This much is clear in reading the text: some people assigned female at birth experience their bodies as other to them. And this much is clear in reading the scholarship surrounding the book: some people assigned female at birth do not or at least wish they do not (such as, to just give one example, Lloyd).

I propose that we approach this difference less as a question of ideology or political stance and more as a question of affect or structures of feeling. Faced with alienation from her body, alienation that very well may be a result of patriarchy, Beauvoir's authorial voice shows signs of a repeated pattern or style of thinking. This is a tendency, a pattern of orientation, a structure of feeling in response to a context.

For example, there are many moments in *The Second Sex* where it seems as though Beauvoir desires a form of embodiment that has not been differentiated for the purposes of reproduction. As Antonopoulos recognizes, *The Second Sex* contends that sexual differentiation is contingent. Beauvoir cites what she calls the "modern theory of sexuality": "In male and female vertebrates, the soma is identical and can be considered a neutral element; the action of the gonad gives its sexual characteristic; some of the secreted hormones act as stimulants and others as inhibitors; the genital tract itself is somatic, and embryology shows that it takes shape under the influence of hormones from bisexual precursors." (2011, 31)

Here, Beauvoir considers the existence of a "neutral" body. Unlike the other scientific accounts that Beauvoir summarizes, she does not explicitly refute this one. Building on this argument, Beauvoir concludes:

> The perpetuation of the species does not entail differentiation. That it is taken on by existents in such a way that it thereby enters into the concrete definition of existence, so be it. Nevertheless, a consciousness without a body or an immortal human being is rigorously inconceivable, whereas a society can be imagined that reproduces itself by parthenogenesis or is composed of herm-aphrodites. (24)

In making this argument, Beauvoir intervenes in the belief that the evolution of "higher species" required and requires "sexual differentiation" (22). This belief, she insists, is "contestable" (23). Sexual differentiation should not be seen as a sign of "evolutionary progress" and its so-called lack has nothing to do with degeneration. In other words, Beauvoir contests the understanding that sexual difference is necessary and a sign of progress, an understanding that has been recently outlined by many, such as Jules Gill-Peterson (2018b) and Kyla Schuller (2018). Doing so, Beauvoir implicitly rejects the use of gendered logics that have promoted racial hierarchies. She imagines a world where production and reproduction do not rely upon sexual difference. "So be it," Beauvoir writes, that sexual differentiation has entered "into the concrete definition of existence" (2011, 24).[22] We can imagine Beauvoir here just saying "*bon*" or "fine" in a somewhat angry tone of resignation. Yes, fine. Sexual differentiation has become part of existence. But this need not be so; it is not necessary and it is not a good in itself. It is, rather, an accident. Existence, including human existence, does not require it. In fact, Beauvoir writes that "cases of intersexuality are numerous in animals and human beings" (30). Reading between the lines, it is not hard to say that the authorial voice wishes that we could move beyond the sexual differentiation that has emerged. This is then a central part of what I am calling a nonbinary structure of feeling in *The Second Sex*: the desire for a nonsexually differentiated human life.

This desire breaks from the valuation of sexual difference and heterosexual marriage as well as the pronatalism of the French Republic. As Camille Robcis explains (2013), there is striking continuity across France's Third Republic, the Vichy regime, Liberation, and the Fourth Republic. Each of these periods (the periods within which Beauvoir grew up and then wrote *The Second Sex*) developed strong pronatalist, family policies that were largely agreed upon by people across the political spectrum. Robcis argues that support for these policies not only followed from concern that French birth rates were declining and therefore that "French families" ought to be encouraged to have "more French babies" (45). Even more central was the place of the heterosexual family in the Republican social contract. In this model, the heterosexual family is understood as a universal structure through which individuals pass in order to enter into the social order. The heterosexual family provides symbolic and psychic order. Robcis traces how this idea developed in French political and intellectual culture through the influence of both Claude Lévi-Strauss and Jacques Lacan. Both thinkers, Robcis explains, insisted on the importance of sexual difference (as expressed either in the incest prohibition or in the Oedipus complex) as a central "catalyst for the transition from nature to society for Lévi-Strauss and as the anchoring of the symbolic for Lacan" (4). These arguments continue to have purchase today, as French society debates the legal and social place of nonnormative families and genders. Because the distinction between

---

[22] "So be it" is a translation of *soit*: "Que celle-ci [la differentiation sexuelle] soit assumée par les existants de telle manière qu'en retour elle entre dans la definition concrète de l'existence, soit" (1949, 40).

nature and culture has been tied to racial hierarchies, the "social" or the "symbolic" order is at once heteronormative and implicated in an imaginary of French racialized "civilization." Thus, although it is clear that Beauvoir certainly does not break from many of the habits of whiteness, and while she is clearly situated as a "French citizen," a Catholic woman of the nation, at the same time, her break from the culture of sexual difference shows some distancing from the project of French "civilization" and a different imaginary of its potential order.

And I share this structure of feeling with Beauvoir. I'm forty-one, and I go to see an OB/GYN to discuss the monthly migraines I suffer. The doctor, who appears queer, offers me the drug norethindrone and explains that on it I will never have to get my period again. I want to repeat that sentence: I would never have to get my period again. *Why did it take until I was forty-one for me to find this freedom?* That is a loaded term, I know. But let me speak frankly: I experience no value in menstruating. I don't like it. It's annoying. It gives me diarrhea. Some months, the migraines it gives me leave me immobile, having me lie in bed, in quiet darkness until I have to vomit. These months, for several days, I cannot do the things that love. I do not have this experience because I value "transcendence" over "immanence," "will" over the "body." Beauvoir's description of menstruation helps me to articulate how menstruation takes me away from those activities and experiences that I love, "simple" activities, activities not necessarily associated with "will" or "transcendence," in fact: eating, feeling sunshine, listening to music. This is embodiment, and menstruation takes me away from my embodied self.

I take the pills (for reasons other than those for which they were developed – they are usually used for birth control) because, as Michelle O'Brien explains of the gender-confirming drugs that she takes, "I like what they do to my body" (2013, 56). This does not make me a dupe of medicine, but it does mean that, like O'Brien, I reject the "crude escapists of eco-primitivism" (64). Rejecting norethindrone will not change how my body is always already entangled in the "structures of transnational capital, the pharmaceutical industries" (57). It is only in a commitment to some ideal "nature" or "purity" that I don't have, that I would choose not to take up the OB/GYN's offer. "I would rather be a cyborg than a goddess" (Haraway, 1991, 181), and biology does not "form a fixed destiny" (Beauvoir, 2011, 44). I cannot but conclude that the fact it has taken me so long to be offered this drug is a form of oppression. Someone out there, many people, and eventually myself thought that me menstruating was "normal" and expected, that I ought to tolerate it, that it was a condition of my existence, that I was not to complain, that it was part of who I was. And so yes, we should counter the shame and stigma associated with menstruation. Yes, we should make menstrual products available in public bathrooms and covered by health insurance. And yes, as Susan Wendell argues, living with pain, fatigue, nausea creates "different *ways of being* that give valuable perspectives on life and the world" (2013, 171). That's true. However, in addition to changing the economic, social, and cultural context of menstruation, we can also make available practices that allow people not to menstruate if they do not want to. I want to give Beauvoir the drugs. In fact, after I discover that menstruation is not necessary, I tell everyone who will listen, and I am surprised. Even some of my lesbian friends claim that they wouldn't want to stop it. They are attached to this experience of their bodies. I don't understand this, but I note the difference.

Beauvoir noticed this divergence too. *Memoirs of a Dutiful Daughter* describes at length Beauvoir's friendship with Zaza. Both girls are raised in similar milieus (for instance, both are sent to the same French Catholic girls' school). Both are smart. Both love philosophy and literature. Beauvoir describes Zaza as vivacious and as having an "independence of spirit" (94). She figures herself as more conservative (94). Yet whereas Beauvoir explains how she never considers "pregnancy and child birth" as part of her "future" (87), Zaza wants to give birth and become a mother. Because of this, I surmise that were Zaza to describe her experience of female embodiment, it would appear significantly different from the biology chapter of *The Second Sex*.

Beauvoir explicitly understands her dissimilarity to Zaza in gendered terms. While Beauvoir insists that she does not "renounce" her femininity (295), she also sees herself as differently gendered from others: "In many respects I set Zaza, my sister . . . above my masculine friends, for they seemed to me more sensitive, more generous, more endowed with imagination, tears, and love. I flattered myself that I combined "a woman's heart and a man's brain." Again I considered myself to be unique – the One and Only." (296)

Here, Beauvoir clearly considers herself as different, neither exactly feminine nor masculine. She is feminine, but also bears traits of masculinity. This is an individualizing feeling (she is "unique – the One and Only"). And this position sets her apart from her friend Zaza, who she so admired. Beauvoir's framework here clearly traffics in gender stereotypes, but what is interesting about it is not the fact that it does but the ways in which it responds to those stereotypes. Faced with traditional gender, Beauvoir sees herself bearing traits related to both women and men, masculinity and femininity. This response, too, is part of a nonbinary structure of feeling: rather than seeking to inhabit a gendered position and striving, perhaps, to remake the meaning of that gender, Beauvoir rather moves between positions, scrambling them.

In fact, while *Memoirs of a Dutiful Daughter* insists that Beauvoir does not reject femininity, *The Second Sex* is less clear. In her essay on biology in *The Second Sex*, Moira Gatens includes this telling sentence: "On Beauvoir's account, it is femininity itself – or, at least, femininity as constituted under oppressive conditions – that should be abandoned" (2003, 277). But which is it? "Femininity itself" or "femininity as constituted under oppressive conditions"? The difference seems important, and the conclusion of *The Second Sex* is ambiguous. Beauvoir argues that "the conflict" between men and women will last "as long as men and women do not recognize each other as peers, that is, as long as femininity is perpetuated as such" (2011, 755). Beauvoir is also disparaging of masculinity, claiming that men are hostile toward women because they are "consumed by the concern to appear male, important, superior" (756). To assume masculinity, man, Beauvoir argues, must alienate "himself in the other" (756). He then becomes afraid of the other, woman, because "he is afraid of the character with whom he is assimilated" (756). This argument anticipates the American, radical feminist approach to gender, developed some twenty years later, which I cannot but read as a sustained argument for the dismantling of gender in toto (e.g., Rubin, 1975; MacKinnon, 1989). But Beauvoir also writes that

> "certain differences between men and woman will always exist; her eroticism, and thus her sexual world, possessing a singular form, cannot fail to engender in her a sensuality, a singular sensitivity: her relation to her body, to the male body, and to the child will never be the same as those man has with his body, with the female body, and with the child" (765).

This passage seems to suggest that Beauvoir calls for a reframing of femininity (and masculinity) such that it is "femininity as constituted under oppressive conditions" that ought to be abandoned, not femininity as such. That is, if there will always be a difference in "men's" and "women's" relationship to their bodies, that difference could become the meaning that is then elaborated in or as femininity and masculinity. Reading along these lines, as Toril Moi puts it, "What Beauvoir wishes to escape is patriarchal femininity, not the fact of being a woman. . . . There is in *The Second Sex* a recognition that women will never be free unless they establish a sense of themselves as female, as well as human" (2008, 228).

On the other hand, Beauvoir seems to say something more than this, as well. The book ends with a turn to "brotherhood." Beauvoir writes: Within the given world, it is up to man to make the reign of freedom triumph; to carry off this supreme victory, men and women must, among other things and beyond their natural differentiations, unequivocally affirm their brotherhood. (766)

Beauvoir here seeks a relation between women and men that exists "beyond their natural differentiations," and that relation is figured as a masculine form of relationality: "brotherhood," a translation of the French term *fraternité*. In this sense, it seems as though it is femininity in general and not femininity merely as it has been constituted that must be abandoned. The world that Beauvoir calls for is the social world of brotherhood. Femininity might be expressed in the private realm of eroticism, but within the "world," it needs to be abandoned for brotherhood.

This call for *fraternité*, as Megan Burke explains, is contentious, often read as complicit with the masculinist a rejection of the feminine (2019, 3–4). Burke contests this view, arguing that Beauvoir imagines a future androgynous world, a world where little girls "were raised with the same demands and honors, the same severity and freedom, as her brothers," where "the mother would enjoy the same lasting prestige as the father" (Beauvoir, 2011, 761). This is not, as Irigaray writes of androgyny, "a utopia of decadents plunged in their own world of fantasy and speculation' (1993b, 123). It also is not a "new society where sex morphology is again suppressed by more or less delusional mental states'" (1993b 123). Instead, in this environment, "the child would feel an androgynous world around her and not a masculine world" (Burke, 2019, 14). Burke argues that *fraternité*, in this vision, is not a masculinist world, but "a new kind of ethical and political relationship in a new kind of world, an androgynous world" (9).

Building on Burke, we can turn to another passage earlier in the conclusion where Beauvoir again insists on the establishment of *fraternité*. Here, Beauvoir calls for a new relationship between men and women, a relationship that begins in the recognition that both suffer "the same drama of flesh and spirit" (2011, 763). Both "are eaten away by time, stalked by death, they have the same essential need of the other; and they can take the same glory from their freedom" (763). Notwithstanding their limits, if they learned how to savor their freedom, "they would no longer be tempted to contend for false privileges; and fraternity would be born between them" (763). In this passage in particular, it seems that while Beauvoir uses the language of *fraternité*, at the same time, this relationality is not masculine in that it is dependent on the mutual recognition of the shared ambiguity of the human condition, which masculinity, by definition, seeks to project onto woman, the Other.

But then why call it *fraternité*? Why would Beauvoir, who understands how the masculine has been used to figure the standard and the universal at the expense of women and who insists that women need to be freed as women, end her text with this turn to *fraternité*? One answer, of course, is that she is a dutiful daughter. This ending asserts her commitment to the nation, France, and her ultimate acceptance of the rhetoric of universalism and abstract individualism at the heart of the Republic (Scott, 2005; Ambroise-Rendu, 2011; Robcis, 2013).

And yet in addition to this interpretation, I venture to add another reading of Beauvoir's calls for *fraternité*. The conclusion of *The Second Sex* highlights a tendency or structure of feeling in the text, a feeling that even if femininity were transformed, the authorial voice would not feel comfortable in it. The voice of the text does not identify with femininity and does not find solace, simply, in its remaking. Beauvoir seeks something else, something more, a form of relationality wherein actors engage beyond their "natural differentiations" (766). This is certainly not to say that femininity should not transform – Beauvoir is clear that it ought to. She is clear that women need to be recognized as subjects, as women. And yet, at the same time, she desires something additional, too, something that hovers in the text and is not necessarily explicit, but that nonetheless exerts its force, in this case, in the apparent contradictions of the conclusion. Quite simply, the voice desires a mode of being and relating to others that is not structured by binary sex.

5.4 A Politics of Contradiction

I have argued that both in *The Second Sex*'s conclusion and in its chapter on biology, especially as read alongside *Memories of a Dutiful Daughter*, we can identify a nonbinary structure of feeling, one that is not explicit but that manifests itself in the tendencies, tone, and even contradictions of the text. This structure of feeling is found in the text's disidentification with female embodiment, its desire for a nonsexually differentiated human life, its longing for a mode of relating that is not structured by binary sex, and its movement between traditional gendered positions and identifications.

This nonbinary structure of feeling should not be read as taking away from the text's feminism, however. Rather, Beauvoir calls for both a feminist and nascently trans (or at least nonbinary) politics, even if the latter is not explicit. The authorial voice asks for both even if there are tensions or contradictions between them. Once again, reading the memoir alongside *The Second Sex* helps me to see this. Strikingly, Beauvoir's memoir concludes with Zaza's death of (it seems) meningitis. Beauvoir ends the book: "She has often appeared to me at night, her face all yellow under a pink sun-bonnet, and seeming to gaze reproachfully at me. We had fought together against the revolting fate that had lain ahead of us, and for a long time I believed that I had paid for my own freedom with her death." (360)

This passage is puzzling. Why ever would Zaza be reproachful of Beauvoir? Jealous, most especially that Beauvoir gets to live, yes, but reproachful? And why is it that Beauvoir might think that she paid for her own freedom with Zaza's death? What is it about Zaza's death that might bring Beauvoir's freedom?

It is telling that Beauvoir ends the book by claiming that both she and her friend fought a "revolting fate," even if Zaza's desires for her future included marriage, pregnancy, and maternity. It seems that for Beauvoir, the revolting fate means not getting to determine one's own projects, not getting to determine one's future, to the extent possible. The question of why Zaza might be reproachful is more difficult to understand. I read this reproach as having to do with Beauvoir's relationship with Sartre. As the memoir describes, a major tension emerges between Zaza and Beauvoir: Zaza keeps her Catholic faith even if Beauvoir turns away from the church, and both have different goals for their future. This raises ethical issues for both young women, Beauvoir contends, and reading through the lines of *Memoirs of a Dutiful Daughter*, it is easy to understand Beauvoir's development of what she calls a "pluralist morality" in response to her relationship with Zaza. She explains that she "cooked up" this philosophy "to accommodate the people I like but whom I didn't want to resemble" (344). This "pluralist morality" can be understood in contrast to Kant's categorical imperative, where one acts in accordance to a law that one wills universal. Breaking from this perspective, Beauvoir's model allows for both Zaza and Beauvoir to pursue their own actions without universalizing their trajectories as the good. Her model allows, in fact, not simply "plurality," but even more strongly, contradiction and opposition.[23]

However, in a key moment early in their relationship, when Beauvoir explains her pluralist position to Sartre, he "demolishes it" (344). Could Beauvoir's feelings of guilt, projected in the figure of the reproachful ghost of Zaza, be the result of her (at least temporary) abandonment of this pluralist morality, a position with which she was able to accommodate the difference between herself and Zaza? Could the abandonment of this morality, one that bears similarities to the feminist ethics of care, be the condition of Beauvoir's relationship with Sartre, a relationship that in Beauvoir's view offers her a level of freedom?

Reading the final passage of the memoir in this way influences my understanding of *The Second Sex*. Say we not let Zaza go, say we understand Zaza's imagined reproach as Beauvoir's own feelings of remorse about turning away from the ethics of plurality – or even, contradiction – could we not then read *The Second Sex* as imagining two different ways to respond to the situation of being

---

[23] Many thanks to my colleague Leigh Mercer for clarifying that this position embraces not simply "plurality" but also (more fundamentally) contradiction.

a woman (and more particularly, a white, Catholic woman) in her contemporary society? Could one way be Zaza's and the other Beauvoir's? Might one model map onto the project of redefining femininity, of developing even an ethics of sexual difference and might the other be the refusal of sexual difference? Beauvoir leaves two possibilities open: one, that woman could transform as woman, that is, "in the feminine condition" she could "accomplish herself" (2011, 16). But another possibility is that that accomplishment might transform the lived body as well, such that one might no longer be a woman, no longer exist in the feminine condition. Instead of picking one approach or another, Beauvoir's feeling in thought calls for both.

References

Alcoff, L. M. (2000). "Merleau-Ponty and Feminist Theory on Experience." In *Chiasms: Merleau-Ponty's Notion of Flesh*, edited by F. Evans and L. Lawlor. Albany: State University of New York Press.

(2015). *The Future of Whiteness*. New York: Polity Press. pp. 251–272.

Allen, S., et al. (2019). "Doing Better in Arguments about Sex, Gender, and Trans Rights." *Medium*. May 23, 2019.

Ambroise-Rendu, A. (2011). "Fraternity." Trans. by A. Goldhammer. In *The French Republic: History, Values, Debates*, edited by E. Bereson, V. Duclear, and C. Prochas. Ithaca: Cornell University Press. pp. 112–118

Amin, K. (2016). "Haunted by the 1990s: Queer Theory's Affective Histories." *Women's Studies Quarterly* 44.3–4:173–189.

(2022). "We Are All Nonbinary: A Brief History of Accidents." *Representations* 158: 106–119.

Anderson, D. (2022). *In Transit: Being Nonbinary in a World of Dichotomies*. New York: Broadleaf Books.

Antonopoulos, A. A. (2017). "Who Is the Subject of *The Second Sex*? Life, Science and Transmasculine Embodiment in Beauvoir's Chapter on Biology." In *A Companion to Simone de Beauvoir*, edited by L. Hengehold and N. Bauer. Oxford: Blackwell. pp. 463–477.

Associated Press. (2017). *The Associated Press Stylebook*. New York: Basic Books.

Awkward-Rich, C. (2017). "Trans, Feminism: Or, Reading like a Depressed Transsexual." *Signs: Journal of Women in Culture and Society* 42.4: 819–841.

Bailey, M. (2021). *Misogynoir Transformed: Black Women's Digital Resistance*. New York: New York University Press.

Barke, M. J., and A. Iantaffi. (2019). *Life Isn't Binary*. London: Jessica Kingsley Publishers.

Barker, J., ed. (2017). *Critically Sovereign*. Durham, NC: Duke University Press.

Beauvoir, S. de (1949). *Le deuxième sexes*. Paris: Gallimard.

(1958). *Mémoires d'une jeune fille rangée*. Paris: Gallimard.

(1974). *Memoirs of a Dutiful Daughter*. Trans. James Kirkup. New York: Harper Colophon Books.

(2011). *The Second Sex*. Trans. C. Borde and S. Malovany-Chevallier. New York: Vintage Books.

Bechdel, A. (2006). *Fun Home: A Family Tragicomic*. Boston: Mariner Books.

Beischel, W., S. Gauvin, and S. van Anders. (2021). "'A Little Shiny Gender Breakthrough': Community Understandings of Gender Euphoria." *International Journal of Transgender Health* 23.3: 1–21.

Benavente, G., and J. Gill-Peterson. (2019). "The Promise of Trans Critique: Susan Stryker's Queer Theory." *GLQ: A Journal of Lesbian and Gay Studies* 25.1: 23–38.

Bergoffen, D. (2003). "Failed Friendships, Forgotten Genealogies." *Bulletin de la Société Américaine de Philosophie de Langue Française* 13.1: 16–31.

Bettcher, T. M. (2009). "Trans Identities and First-Person Authority." In *You've Changed: Sex Reassignment and Personal Identity*, edited by L. Shrage. Oxford: Oxford University Press. pp. 98–120.

Binnie, I. (2013). *Nevada*. New York: Topside Press.

Bond Stockton, K. (2009). *The Queer Child, or Growing Sideways in the Twentieth Century*. Durham, NC: Duke University Press.

Bornstein, K. (1994). *Gender Outlaw*. New York: Routledge.

boyd, d. (2011). "Social Network Sites as Networked Publics: Affordances, Dynamics, and Implications." In *A Networked Self*, edited by Z. Papacharissi. New York: Routledge. pp. 39–58.

Brewer, M. (2007). "*Peter Pan* and the White Imperial Imaginary." *New Theater Quarterly* 23.4: 387–392.

Brown, S. (2015). *Dark Matters: On the Surveillance of Blackness*. Durham, NC: Duke University Press.

Brown, W. (2015). *Undoing the Demos: Neoliberalism's Stealth Revolution*. Princeton, NJ: Zone Books.

Butler, J. (1990). *Gender Trouble: Feminism and the Subversion of Identity*. New York: Routledge.

Burke, M. (2019). "Beauvoirian Androgyny: Reflections on the Androgynous World of Fraternité in *The Second Sex*." *Feminist Theory* 20.1: 3–18.

(2020). "On Bad Faith and Authenticity: Rethinking Genderless Subjectivity." *Simone de Beauvoir Studies* 31: 86–104.

Byron, P. (2021). *Digital Media, Friendship and Cultures of Care*. New York: Routledge.

Califia, P. (1997). *Sex Changes: The Politics of Transgenderism*. San Francisco: Cleis.

cárdenas, m. (2016). "Trans of Color Poetics: Stitching Bodies, Concepts, and Algorithms." *S&F Online* 13.3:14.1.

(2017). "Dark Shimmers: The Rhythm of Necropolitical Affect in Digital Media." In *Trap Door: Trans Cultural Production and the Politics of*

Visibility, edited by R. Gossett, E. A. Stanley, and J. Burton. Cambridge: MIT Press. pp.161–183.

Cavalcante, A. (2016). "'I Did It All Online': Transgender Identity and the Management of Everyday Life." *Critical Studies in Media Communications* 33.1: 109–122.

Cheah, P., E. Grosz, J. Butler, and D. Cornell, (1998). "The Future of Sexual Difference: An Interview with Judith Butler and Drucilla Cornell." *Diacritics* 28.1: 19–42.

Chen, J. N. (2019). *Trans Exploits: Trans of Color Critique and Technologies in Movement*. Durham, NC: Duke University Press.

Chen, M. (2017). "Everywhere Archives: Transgender, Trans Asians, and the Internet." In *Trap Door: Trans Cultural Production and the Politics of Visibility*, edited by R. Gossett, E. A. Stanley, and J. Burton. Cambridge: MIT Press. pp. 147–160.

Cho, A. (2017). "Default Publicness: Queer Youth of Color, Social Media, and Being Outed by the Machine." *New Media & Society* 20.9: 3183–3200.

Chu, A. L. (2019). *Females*. New York: Verso.

Chu, A. L., and E. H. Drager. (2019). "After Trans Studies." *TSQ: Transgender Studies Quarterly* 6.1: 103–116.

Clare, S. (2017). "'Finally, She's Accepted Herself!': Coming Out in Neoliberal Times." *Social Text* 35.2: 17–38.

Dame-Griff, A. (2019). "Herding the 'Performing Elephants': Using Computational Methods to Study Usenet." *Internet Histories* 3.3–4: 223–244.

(2020). "Trans Cultures Online." *The International Encyclopedia of Gender*. Wiley Online Library.

Decena, C. U. (2008). "Tacit Subjects." *GLQ: Journal of Lesbian and Gay Studies* 14.2–3: 339–359.

De Ridder, S., and S. Van Bauwel. (2015). "The Discursive Construction of Gay Teenagers in Times of Mediatization: Youth's Reflections on Intimate Storytelling, Queer Shame and Realness in Popular Social Media Places." *Journal of Youth Studies* 18.6: 777–793.

Dobson, A. S., B. Robards, and N. Carah. (2018). "Digital Intimate Publics and Social Media: Toward Theorising Public Lives on Private Platforms." In *Digital Intimate Publics and Social Media*, edited by A. S. Dobson, B. Robards, and N. Carah. Cham, Switzerland: Palgrave Macmillan. pp. 3–27.

Duclos, V., and T. S. Criado. (2019). "Care in Trouble: Ecologies of Support from Below and Beyond." *Medical Anthropology Quarterly* 34.2: 153–173.

Dyer, R. (1997). *White: Essays on Race and Culture*. New York: Routledge.

Elliott, J. (2006). "The Currency of Feminist Theory." *PMLA* 121.5: 1697–1703.

Fanon, F. ([1952] 2008). *Black Skin, White Masks*. Trans. C. Lam Markmann. London: Pluto Press.

Feinberg, L. (1996). *Transgender Warriors*. Boston: Beacon Press.

(1998). *Trans Liberation: Beyond Pink or Blue*. Boston: Beacon Press.

Ferguson, R. (2003). *Aberrations in Black: Toward a Queer of Color Critique*. Minneapolis: University of Minnesota Press.

Foucault, M. (1988). *The History of Sexuality, Volume 3: The Care of the Self*. Trans. by R. Hurley. Vintage: New York.

(1990). *The History of Sexuality, Volume 1: The Will to Knowledge*. Trans. by R. Hurley. Harmondsworth: Penguin.

(1995). *Discipline and Punish: The Birth of the Prison*. Trans. by A Sheridan. New York: Vintage Books.

(2008). *The Birth of Biopolitics: Lectures at the Collège De France, 1978–79*. New York: Palgrave Macmillan.

Gatens, M. (2003). "Beauvoir and Biology: A Second Look." In *The Cambridge Companion to Simone de Beauvoir*, edited by C. Card. New York: Cambridge University Press. pp. 266–287.

Gearhardt, N. (2019). "Rethinking Trans History and Gay History in Early Twentieth-Century New York." *QED: A Journal in GLBTQ Worldmaking* 6.1: 26–47.

Gill-Peterson, J. (2018a). *Histories of the Transgender Child*. Minneapolis: University of Minnesota Press.

(2018b). "Trans of Color Critique Before Transsexuality." *TSQ: Transgender Studies Quarterly* 5.4 (November): 606–620.

Gilman, S. (1985). "Black Bodies, White Bodies: Toward an Iconography of Female Sexuality in Late Nineteenth-Century Art, Medicine, and Literature." *Critical Inquiry* 12.1: 204–242.

Ginelle, L. (2014). "TERF War: The New Yorker's One-Sided Article Undermines Transgender Identity." *Bitch Media*. August 1, 2014.

Goldberg, M. (2014). "What Is a Woman: The Dispute Between Radical Feminism and Transgenderism." *New York Times*. July 28, 2014.

Gossett, R., E. A. Stanley, and J. Burton. (2017). "Known Unknowns: An Introduction to *Trap Door*." In *Trap Door: Trans Cultural Production and the Politics of Visibility*, edited by R. Gossett, E. A. Stanley, and J. Burton. Cambridge: MIT Press. pp. xv–xxvi.

Grosz, E. (1994). *Volatile Bodies: Toward a Corporeal Feminism*. Bloomington: Indiana University Press.

(2011). *Becoming Undone: Darwinian Reflections on Life, Politics, and Art.* Durham, NC: Duke University Press.

Guy-Sheftall, B. (1990). *Daughters of Sorrow: Attitudes Toward Black Women, 1880–1920.* Brooklyn, NY: Carlson.

Halberstam, J. (1994). "F2 M: The Making of Female Masculinity." In *The Lesbian Postmodern*, edited by L. Doan. New York: Columbia University Press. pp. 210–228.

(1998). "Transgender Butch: Butch/FTM Border Wars and the Masculine Continuum." *GLQ: A Journal of Lesbian and Gay Studies* 4.2: 287–310.

(2020). "Nice Trannies." *TSQ: Transgender Studies Quarterly* 7.3: 321–331.

Hale, J. (1998). "Consuming the Living, Dis(re)membering the Dead in the Butch/FTM Borderlands." *GLQ: A Journal of Lesbian and Gay Studies* 4.2: 311–348

(2009). "Suggested Rules for Non-transsexuals Writing about Transsexuals, Transsexuality, or Trans ____." Last updated November 18, 2009. http://sandystone.com/hale.rules.html.

Hammonds, E. (1997). "Toward a Genealogy of Black Female Sexuality: The Problematic of Silence." In *Feminist Genealogies, Colonial Legacies, Democratic Futures*, edited by J. Alexander and C. T. Mohanty. New York: Routledge. pp. 170–182.

Hanhardt, C. B. (2013). *Safe Space: Gay Neighborhood History and the Politics of Violence.* Durham, NC: Duke University Press.

Haraway, D. (1991). *Simians, Cyborgs, and Women: The Reinvention of Nature.* New York: Routledge.

Haritaworn, J., and C. Riley Snorton. (2013). "Trans Necropolitics: A Transnational Reflection on Violence, Death, and Trans of Color Afterlife." In *The Transgender Studies Reader*, edited by S. Stryker and A. Aizura. New York: Routledge. pp. 65–76.

Harris, C. (1993). "Whiteness as Property." *Harvard Law Review* 106.8: 1710–1791.

Hausman, B. (1995). *Changing Sex: Transsexualism, Technology, and the Idea of Gender.* Durham, NC: Duke University Press.

Heaney, E. (2017). *The New Woman: Literary Modernism, Queer Theory, and the Trans Feminine Allegory.* Evanston, IL: Northwestern University Press.

Heïnemaa, S. (2003). "The Body as Instrument and Expression." In *The Cambridge Companion to Simone de Beauvoir*, edited by C. Card. Cambridge: Cambridge University Press. pp. 66–86.

Hekman, S. (1990). *Gender and Knowledge: Elements of a Postmodern Feminism.* New York: Polity Press.

Hines, S. (2019). "The Feminist Frontier: On Trans and Feminism." *Journal of Gender Studies* 28.2: 145–157.

Hobart H. J. K., and T. Kneese. (2020). "Radical Care: Survival Strategies for Uncertain Times." *Social Text* 38.1: 1–16.

Hong, G. K. (2015). *Death Beyond Disavowal: The Impossible Politics of Difference*. Minneapolis: University of Minnesota Press.

Illouz, E. (2007). *Cold Intimacies: The Making of Emotional Capitalism*. Oxford: Polity Press.

Irigaray, L. (1980). "When Our Lips Speak Together." Trans. C. Burke. *Signs: Journal of Women in Culture and Society* 6.1: 69–79.

(1992). *Je, tu, nous: Pour une culture de la différence*. Paris: Le livre de poche.

(1993a). *An Ethics of Sexual Difference*. Trans. by C. Burke and G. Gill. Ithaca, NY: Cornell University Press.

(1993b). *Sexes and Genealogies*. Trans. G. Gill. New York: Columbia University Press.

Jeffreys, S. (2014). *Gender Hurts: A Feminist Analysis of the Politics of Transgenderism* London: Routledge.

Jones, C., and J. Slater. (2020). "The Toilet Debate: Stalling Trans Possibilities and Defending Women's Protected Spaces." *Sociological Review Monographs* 68.4: 834–851.

Katz, J. (1976). *Gay American History: Lesbian and Gay Men in the USA*. Ann Arbor: University of Michigan Press.

Koyoma, E. (2003). "The Transfeminist Manifesto." In *Catching a Wave: Reclaiming Feminism for the Twenty-First Century*, edited by R. Dicker and A. Piepmeier. Boston: Northeastern University Press. pp. 244–262.

Kristeva, J. (1995). *Maladies of the Soul*. Trans. by R. Guberman. New York: Columbia University Press.

Lawford-Smith, H. (2022). *Gender-Critical Feminism*. Oxford: Oxford University Press.

Léon, C. T. (1988). "Simone de Beauvoir's Woman: Eunuch or Male?" *Ultimate Reality of Meaning* 11: 196–211.

Lloyd, G. (1984). *The Man of Reason: "Male" and "Female" in Western Philosophy*. Minneapolis: University of Minnesota Press.

Lugones, M. (2007). "Heterosexualism and the Colonial/Modern Gender System." *Hypatia* 22.1: 186–209.

MacKinnon, C. (1989). *Toward a Feminist Theory of the State*. Cambridge, MA: Harvard University Press.

Macpherson, C. B. (1962). *The Political Theory of Possessive Individualism: Hobbes to Locke*. Oxford: Clarendon Press.

Malatino, H. (2020). *Trans Care*. Minneapolis: University of Minnesota Press.

Marcus, S., and S. Best. (2009). "Surface Reading: An Introduction." *Representations* 108.1: 1–21.

Marhoefer, L. (2022). *Racism and the Making of Gay Rights: A Sexologist, His Student, and the Empire of Queer Love*. Toronto: University of Toronto Press.

Marvin, A. (2019). "Groundwork for Transfeminist Care Ethics: Sara Ruddick, Trans Children, and Solidarity in Dependency." *Hypatia* 34.1: 101–120.

McCune, J. (2014). *Sexual Discretion: Black Masculinity and the Politics of Passing*. Chicago: University of Chicago Press.

McMullin, D. (2011). "Fa'afafine Notes: On Tagaloa, Jesus, and Nafanua." In *Queer Indigenous Studies*, edited by Q. Driskill, C. Finley, B. J. Gilley, and S. L. Morgensen. Tucson: University of Arizona Press. pp. 81–96.

Melamed, J. (2011). *Represent and Destroy: Rationalizing Violence in the New Racial Capitalism*. Minneapolis: University of Minnesota Press.

Moi, T. (2008). *What Is a Woman? And Other Essays*. New York: Oxford University Press.

(1986). "Existentialism and Feminism: The Rhetoric of Biology in *The Second Sex*." *Oxford Literary Review* 8.1: 88–95.

Muñoz, J. E. (2009). *Cruising Utopia: The Then and There of Queer Futurity*. New York: New York University Press.

(2020). *The Sense of Brown*, edited by J. Chambers-Letson and T. Nyong'o. Durham, NC: Duke University Press.

Murphy, M. (2015). "Unsettling Care: Troubling Transnational Itineraries of Care in Feminist Health Practices." *Social Studies of Science* 45.5: 717–737.

Namaste, V. (2000). "'Tragic Misreadings': Queer Theory's Erasure of Transgender Subjectivity." In *Invisible Lives: The Erasure of Transsexual and Transgendered People*, Chicago: University of Chicago Press. pp. 9–23.

(2005). *Sex Change, Social Change: Reflections on Identity, Institutions, and Imperialism*. Toronto: Women's Press.

(2009). "Undoing Theory: The 'Transgender Question' and the Epistemic Violence of Anglo-American Feminist Theory." *Hypatia* 24.3: 11–32.

Nance, T. (2018). "Two Piece and a Biscuit." *Random Acts of Flyness*, Season 1, Episode 2. HBO.

Noble, B. (2006). *Sons of the Movement: FTMs Risking Incoherence on a Post-Queer Cultural Landscape*. Toronto: The Women's Press.

Noddings, N. (1995). "Caring." In *Justice and Care: Essential Readings in Feminist Ethics*, edited by V. Held. New York: Routledge. pp. 7–30.

O'Brien, M. (2013). "Tracing This Body: Transsexuality, Pharmaceuticals and Capitalism." In *The Transgender Studies Reader 2*. edited by S. Stryker and A. Aizura. New York: Routledge. pp. 56–65.

Okely, J. (1986). *Simone de Beauvoir*. New York: Pantheon.

Piepzna-Samarasinha, L. L. (2018). *Care Work: Dreaming Disability Justice*. Vancouver, BC: Arsenal Pulp Press.

Prosser, J. (1998). *Second Skins: The Body Narratives of Transsexuality*. New York: Columbia University Press.

Puar, J. (2007). *Terrorist Assemblages*. Durham, NC: Duke University Press

Rajunov, M., and S. Duane. (2021). *Nonbinary: Memoirs of Gender and Identity*. New York: Columbia University Press.

Rankine, C. (2020). *Just Us: An American Conversation*. Minneapolis: Greywolf Press.

Rankine, C., and J. Lucas. (2020). *Situation 11*. CC:World. https://ccworld .hkw.de/situation-11/.

Rich, A. (1994). *Blood, Bread, and Poetry*. New York: W. W. Norton.

Rifkin, M. (2010). *When Did Indians Become Straight?: Kinship, the History of Sexuality, and Native Sovereignty*. Oxford: Oxford University Press.

Riggs, M. (1989). *Tongues Untied*. San Francisco, CA: California Newsreel.

Robcis, C. (2013). *The Law of Kinship: Anthropology, Psychoanalysis, and the Family in France*. Ithaca, NY: Cornell University Press.

Rubin, G. (1975). "The Traffic in Women: Notes on the 'Political Economy' of Sex." In *Toward an Anthropology of Women*, edited by R. R. Reiter. New York: Monthly Review Press. pp. 157–210.

Rubin, H. (1998). "Phenomenology as Method in Trans Studies." *GLQ: A Journal of Lesbian and Gay Studies* 4.2: 263–281.

Rustin, S. (2020). "Feminist Like Me Aren't Anti-Trans—We Just Can't Discard the Idea of 'Sex.'" *Guardian*, September 30, 2020. https://www .theguardian.com/commentisfree/2020/sep/30/feminists-anti-trans-idea-sex-gender-oppression

Salamon, G. (2010). *Assuming a Body: Transgender and Rhetorics of Materiality*. New York: Columbia University Press.

Schuller, K. (2018). *The Biopolitics of Feeling: Race, Sex, and Science in the Nineteenth Century*. Durham, NC: Duke University Press.

Scott, J. W. (2005). *Parité! Sexuality Equality and the Crisis of French Universalism*. Chicago: University of Chicago Press.

Sedgwick, E. K. (1990). *Epistemology of the Closet*. Berkeley: University of California Press.

(2003). *Touching Feeling: Affect, Pedagogy, Performativity*. Durham, NC: Duke University Press.

Serano, J. (2007). *Whipping Girl: A Transsexual Woman on Sexism and the Scapegoating of Femininity*. Emeryville, CA: Seal Press.

Sharrow, E., and I. Sederbaum. (2022). "Texas Isn't the Only State Denying Essential Medical Care to Trans Youths." *Washington Post*, March 10, 2022. https://www.washingtonpost.com/politics/2022/03/10/texas-trans-kids-abortion-lgbtq-gender-ideology/

Shrier, A. (2020). *Irreversible Damage: The Transgender Craze Seducing Our Daughters*. Washington, DC: Regnery.

shuster, s. (2021). *Trans Medicine: The Emergence and Practice of Treating Gender*. New York: New York University Press.

Snorton, C. R. (2014). *Nobody Is Supposed to Know: Black Sexuality on the Down Low*. Minneapolis: University of Minnesota Press.

(2017). *Black on Both Sides: A Racial History of Trans Identity*. Minneapolis: University of Minnesota Press.

Spade, D. (2006). "Mutilating Gender." *The Transgender Studies Reader*, edited by S. Stryker and S. Whittle. New York: Routledge. pp. 315–332.

Srnicek, N. (2016). *Platform Capitalism*. New York: John Wiley & Sons.

Stock, K. (2018). "Arguing about Feminism and Transgenderism: An Opinionated Guide for the Perplexed." *Medium*. May 18, 2018.

Stone, S. (1992). "The Empire Strikes Back: A Posttranssexual Manifesto." *Camera Obscura* 10.2: 150–176.

Stryker, S. (1994). "My Words to Victor Frankenstein Above the Village of Chamounix." *GLQ: A Journal of Lesbian and Gay Studies* 1: 237–254.

(2004). "Transgender Studies: Queer Theory's Evil Twin." *GLQ: A Journal of Lesbian and Gay Studies* 10.2: 212–215.

(2017). *Transgender History*. Berkeley: Seal Press.

Taylor, C. (2005). "Alternatives to Confession: Foucault's 'Fragments of an Autobiography.'" *Symposium* 9.1: 55–66.

Tronto, J. (1995). "Care as a Basis for Radical Political Judgments." *Hypatia* 10.2: 141–149.

Truitt, J. (2014). "Why *The New Yorker*'s Radical Feminism and Transgenderism Piece Was One-Sided." *Columbia Journalism Review*. August 6, 2014. https://archives.cjr.org/minority_reports/new_yorker_feminism_transgenderism_jos_truitt.php

University of Chicago Press. (2017). *The Chicago Manual of Style*, 17th ed. Chicago: University of Chicago Press.

Vaid-Menon, A. (2020). *Beyond the Gender Binary*. New York: Penguin Random House.

Van Dijck, J. (2013). *The Culture of Connectivity: A Critical History of Social Media*. New York: Oxford University Press.

Ward, J. (2020). *The Tragedy of Heterosexuality*. New York: New York University Press.

Wendell, S. (2013). "Unhealthy Disabled: Treating Chronic Illnesses as Disabilities." In *The Disability Studies Reader*, 4th ed., edited by L. J. Davis. New York: Routledge. pp. 161–176.

Wiegman, R., and E. Wilson. (2015), "Introduction: Antinormativity's Queer Conventions." *Differences* 26.1: 1–25.

Wilchins, R. (2017). "Get to Know the New Pronouns: They, Theirs, and Them." *Advocate*. March 13, 2017. https://www.advocate.com/commen tary/2017/3/13/get-know-new-pronouns-they-theirs-and-them

Williams, R. (1977). *Marxism and Literature*. Oxford: Oxford University Press.

Winnubst, S. (2015). *Way Too Cool: Selling Out Race and Ethics*. New York: Columbia University Press.

Woodward, K. (1988). "Simone de Beauvoir: Aging and Its Discontents." In *The Private Self: Theory and Practice of Women's Autobiographical Writing*, edited by S. Benstock. Chapel Hill: University of North Carolina Press. pp. 90–113.

(2018). "Rereading Simone de Beauvoir's *The Coming of Age*." *Age/Culture/ Humanities: An Interdisciplinary Journal* 3: 191–206.

Wynter, S. (2003). "Unsettling the Coloniality of Being/Power/Truth/Freedom: Towards the Human, After Man, Its Overrepresentation—An Argument." *CR: The New Centennial Review* 3.3: 257–337.

Young, E. (2019). *They/Them/Their: A Guide to Nonbinary and Genderqueer Identities*. London: Jessica Kingsley.

Zimman, L., and W. Hayworth. (2020). "How We Got Here: Short-Scale Change in Identity Labels for Trans, Cis, and Nonbinary People in the 2000s." *Proceedings of the Linguistic Society of America* 5.1: 499–513.

Acknowledgment

Many thanks to Amber Jamilla Musser, Juno Jill Richards, Jennifer Cooks, Laurie Marhoefer, Megan Burke, Anis Bawarshi, April Clark, Mac Murray, Sora Hong, Ingrid Ireland, and Maxine Savage for their help with this project. The manuscript was completed with support from The Walter Chapin Simpson Center for the Humanities and the University of Washington's Royalty Research Fund.

Cambridge Elements ≡

Feminism and Contemporary Critical Theory

Jennifer Cooke
Loughborough University

Jennifer Cooke is Reader in Contemporary Literature and Theory at Loughborough University. She's author of *Contemporary Feminist Life-Writing: The New Audacity* (2020) and editor of *The New Feminist Literary Studies* (2020), *Scenes of Intimacy: Reading, Writing and Theorizing Contemporary Literature* (2013), and a special issue of Textual Practice on challenging intimacies and psychoanalysis (September 2013). Her first monograph is *Legacies of Plague in Literature, Theory and Film* (2009). Her research interests lie in theories of intimacy, the affective turn and theories of the emotions, queer and feminist theories, and contemporary literature. She chaired the Gendered Lives Research Group from 2015–2020.

Amber Jamilla Musser
CUNY Graduate Center

Amber Jamilla Musser is Professor of English at the CUNY Graduate Center. She is the author of *Sensational Flesh: Race, Power, and Masochism* (2014), *Sensual Excess: Queer Femininity and Brown Jouissance* (2018), and co-editor with Kadji Amin and Roy Peréz of a special issue of ASAP Journal on Queer Form (May 2017). She has also published extensively, including essays in *Feminist Theory, differences, Social Text, GLQ, and Women and Performance* on the intersections of critical race theory, sexuality studies, queer of color critique, black feminisms and aesthetics.

Juno Jill Richards
Yale University

Juno Jill Richards is Associate Professor in English and affiliated faculty in Women, Gender, & Sexuality Studies at Yale University. They are the author of *The Fury Archives: Female Citizenship, Human Rights, and the International Avant-Gardes* (2020) and a coauthor of *The Ferrante Letters: An Experiment in Collective Criticism* (2020). Their research focuses on queer/trans archives, social reproduction, critical legal theory, queer feminist science studies, disability justice, and 20/21st-century literature.

About the Series

Elements in Feminism and Contemporary Critical Theory provides a forum for interdisciplinary feminist scholarship that speaks directly to the contemporary moment. Grounded in queer, trans, antiracist, and intersectional feminist traditions, the series expands familiar paradigms of academic writing, locating new methods and modes to account for transformational feminist politics today.

Cambridge Elements $\equiv$

Feminism and Contemporary Critical Theory

Printed in the United States
by Baker & Taylor Publisher Services